ISRAEL
A SACRED LAND

DISCOVERING
our HERITAGE

by Emily Taitz & Sondra Henry

ᒍ‍P DILLON PRESS, INC.
Minneapolis, Minnesota 55415

Acknowledgments

We would like to thank the following people for the photographs included in this book: Robert Fried (© 1987, cover and pages 8, 23, 97); Edward I. Henry, M.D.; Isaac Taitz; Ari Taitz; Rob Fields; Hadassah archivists Ira Daly and Leonard Geller, pages 33, 34, 48, 50, 55, 58, 60, 65, 67, 70, 119; Dina Chertow and Robert Lepsong, Interns for Peace, page 132; Jeff Kreiger and Dolores Mooradian, Committee for Sports in Israel, page 125; Rabbi Chuck Diamond, Temple Israel Hebrew High School, page 14; Lily Rivlin and Ursula Abrams, New Israel Fund, New York; Deborah Manuel, ICM Artists; Christian Steiner, IMG Artists; Danny Ackerman; David Kaplan; Joel Sweet.

We would also like to thank the following people for their assistance in helping us to understand the many different aspects of life in Israel: Kenaan Ben Hayyim, Information Office of the Israel Consulate; Ilit Ben Yosef, New York; Elaine Blankstein, Jerusalem, Israel; Dina Chertow, Interns for Peace, New York office; Rabbi Bruce Cohen, head of Israel office, Interns for Peace; Rachel Donner, teacher at Golda Meir school, Holon, Israel; Tzvia Ginor, poet, New York and Tel Aviv, Israel; Rachel Harmeli, Hertzlia Pituah, Israel; Islamic Center, Washington, D.C.; Walid Mullah, Yarkah, Israel; Judy Pearl, New York; Eva Sussman, New York and Jerusalem, Israel; Isaac Taitz, New York; Ina and Al Yablon, PIP Instant Press, Westbury, New York, for their technical assistance and generosity; Eva Yarett, librarian at Temple Israel Youth House Library, Great Neck, New York, for research assistance; Robbie Young, New York and Israel.

Library of Congress Cataloging in Publication Data

Taitz, Emily.
   Israel : a sacred land.

   (Discovering our heritage)
   Bibliography: p.
   Includes index.
   Summary: Describes the land and people of Israel today and explains the history of the Jews, Arabs, and Christians who have lived there in the past.
   1. Israel—Juvenile literature. [1. Israel] I. Henry, Sondra. II. Title. III. Series.
DS102.95.T34   1987   956.94'054   87-13449
ISBN 0-87518-364-6

Dillon Press, Inc., 242 Portland Avenue South
Minneapolis, Minnesota 55415

Printed in the United States of America
1 2 3 4 5 6 7 8 9 10 96 95 94 93 92 91 90 89 88 87

Contents

Fast Facts About Israel   4

Map of Israel   6

1 The Many Faces of Israel   7

2 A Dream of Peace 28

3 An Old New Land 38

4 Everything Will Be Okay 69

5 Happy Holidays 79

6 Blessed Are They Who Come 96

7 Wake Up! It's Time for School 112

8 Sports is a Common Language 124

9 Those Who Go Down 136

   *Appendix: Israeli Consulates in the
                 United States and Canada* 147

Glossary 149

Selected Bibliography 154

Index 156

Fast Facts About Israel

Official Name: *Medinat Yisra-el* ("The State of Israel").

Capital: Jerusalem.

Location: Israel is a tiny triangular land "bridge" located in the southeast corner of the Mediterranean Sea. It is part of the continent of Asia. Israel shares land borders with Lebanon and Syria to the north, Jordan to the east, and Egypt to the southwest. The lowest point of the triangle borders the Red Sea.

Area: Since Israel has fought many wars, its exact borders have changed several times. In 1987 the country measured 8,430 square miles (21,576 square kilometers). With the occupied, or administered, areas of the West Bank and Gaza included, the entire area governed by Israel is 10,840 square miles (27,817 square kilometers). *Greatest Distances:* north-south—256 miles (412 kilometers); east-west—81 miles (130 kilometers). *Coastline:* Mediterranean—143 miles (230 kilometers).

Elevation: *Highest*—Mount Meron, 3,963 feet (1,208 meters) above sea level; *Lowest*—shore of the Dead Sea, about 1,310 feet (399 meters) below sea level.

Population: 4,131,000 (1987 estimate); *Distribution*—87 percent urban, 13 percent rural; *Density*—488 persons per square mile (188 per square kilometer).

Form of Government: Israel is a parliamentary democracy with one legislative body, the *Knesset*, and a prime minister at its head. Members of the Knesset are representatives of individual political parties and are elected to serve four-year terms. The party with the most votes selects the prime minister.

Important Products: *Agriculture*—citrus fruits, flowers, avocados, tomatoes, strawberries, melons, and cotton. *Industry*—chemicals and fertilizers, polished diamonds, high technology products for irrigation, computers, telecommunications, and medical electronics; also military equipment, textiles, and clothing.

Basic Unit of Money: Shekel.

Major Languages: Hebrew; Arabic and English are also official languages.

Major Religions: Judaism, Islam, Christianity, Druze.

Flag: A ground of white with two horizontal blue stripes on the top and bottom, and a six-pointed star in the center.

National Anthem: *Ha-Tikvah* ("The Hope").

Major Holidays: Jewish New Year and the Day of Atonement (September/October or the first and tenth days of the month of *Tishrei*); Passover (March/April or the fifteenth day of the month of *Nissan*), Sukkot (September/October or the fifteenth day of *Tishrei*); and Shavuot (May/June or fifty days after Passover); Israel Independence Day (May or the fifth day of *Iyyar*).

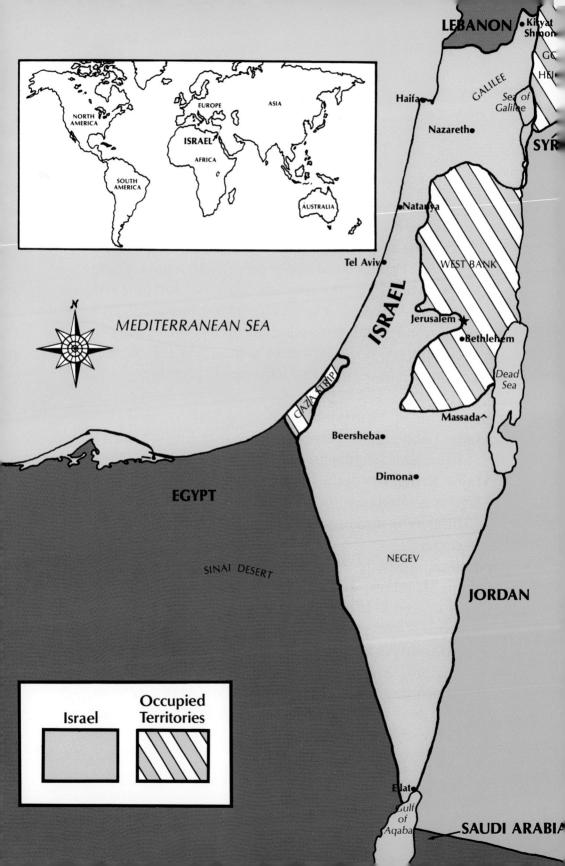

LEBANON

Kiryat Shmon

GO
HEI

GALILEE

Sea of Galilee

SYR

Haifa

Nazareth

NORTH
AMERICA

EUROPE

ASIA

ISRAEL

AFRICA

SOUTH
AMERICA

AUSTRALIA

Natanya

ISRAEL

Tel Aviv

WEST BANK

N

MEDITERRANEAN SEA

Jerusalem

Bethlehem

Dead
Sea

GAZA STRIP

Massada^

Beersheba

EGYPT

Dimona

SINAI DESERT

NEGEV

JORDAN

Occupied
Territories

Israel

Elat

Gulf
of
Aqaba

SAUDI ARABIA

1. The Many Faces of Israel

In the old city of Jerusalem, located almost in the middle of Israel, people of all races, religions, and nationalities mingle in the winding streets. Jewish women and children in modern clothes carry plastic shopping baskets as they walk alongside Arab women in long, embroidered dresses. The Muslim women cover their faces with heavy veils, and they carry baskets of grapes on their heads. Beside them walk Greek Orthodox priests in long black robes and pointed hats, native born "sabra" teenagers with open shirt collars and tan shorts, and *Hasidic* Jews who wear black coats, white stockings, and fur hats even in the hottest weather.

Everyone comes to the "old city," as the Israelis call that ancient section of Jerusalem. They come to shop, to pray at its many shrines—holy to Christians, Jews, and Muslims—and just to look. Visitors from all over the world like to wander down the narrow cobblestoned streets. Here you can buy a great variety of products, from freshly baked round bread called *pita*, to little statues carved from olive wood.

At the city gates Arab women sell grape or mint leaves in bunches, and big black figs from large straw baskets. Through the crowded streets, young Arab boys

In the old city of Jerusalem, a shopkeeper talks with a man who has stopped at his fresh fruit stand.

pull little gray donkeys, men inch along on motor scooters, and women hold net bags bulging with fresh fruit and vegetables.

Israel is a small nation with many different kinds of people. As in Jerusalem, the capital, a wonderful variety of languages, styles, religions, and daily customs exist side by side within this tiny bridge of land connecting

Europe, Asia, and Africa. Some parts of the country are so narrow that it takes less than an hour to drive from the Mediterranean Sea on the west, to the eastern border that Israel shares with Jordan, one of its neighbors.

The Land, Seas, and Seasons

Within Israel there are not only many kinds of people, but also widely different landscapes and climates. To the north in the Galilee region, green hills, valleys, and small ponds for raising fish cover the land. Here it can get very cold in the winter, but summers are long and dry. The Galilee has many trees, and in springtime, wildflowers blanket the hills with patches of red and yellow.

The Sea of Galilee, also called Lake Kinneret because it is shaped like a harp—*kinor* in Hebrew—is the only freshwater lake in Israel. It is located in the Galilee. Modern engineering has brought water from Lake Kinneret to farms and desert areas throughout Israel.

If you stand on a mountain in the northern Galilee, you can look right over Israel's northern border into Syria or Lebanon. To the west and south, along Israel's Mediterranean coast, lie beautiful, sandy beaches and large, modern cities with tall white buildings. Throughout the country it is usually warm enough for swimming at least six months of the year.

The Galilee region in northern Israel has many orchards and farms among its hills and valleys. Before the twentieth century, most of this area was swampland. Then early Jewish pioneers drained and cultivated the land.

The Dead Sea, a large saltwater lake in the Negev Desert area, makes the surrounding land so salty that nothing grows in it.

In the southern part of this small country, there is a rocky desert, which the Israelis call *Negev,* meaning "dry place." Here, it almost never rains. The lowest place on earth—the Dead Sea—fills a part of this desert area. The ground around the Dead Sea is so dry and salty that nothing can grow. Not very far away, though, green oases watered by underground springs form fertile islands in the desert. Here are graceful palms with clusters of dates hanging from the branches, and green fig trees with large shiny leaves. Beyond the Negev to the southwest is the Sinai Desert, which belongs to Egypt.

The People of Israel

Yet in spite of all this variety of culture and scenery, the majority of Israel's people—almost three million of them—are Jews. These Jews have come from seventy countries all over the world. Those from nations such as France, Russia, and Australia look very much like the fair-skinned people of those countries. Dark-skinned, black-haired Jews come from India, Kurdestan, Libya, Morocco, Abyssinia, Afghanistan, and Ethiopia.

A great many Jews came to Israel beginning in the early years of the twentieth century. They spoke different languages and ate different foods. Still, they did have some important things in common. They shared the same religion, prayed in the same language—Hebrew— and held a common belief that the Jews were a nation with their own land.

After Israel became a country, about 50,000 Jews from Yemen, a Middle Eastern land, decided to leave their homes and come there. When they heard about the new Jewish nation, they crossed the desert on foot and then were flown in large transport planes to Israel.

For these Jews, who were very religious, this journey was thought to be the fulfillment of a promise. The Bible had said "They that wait upon the Lord shall mount with wings as eagles." For the Yemenite Jews, the airplanes were the wings of eagles. The Jews in Israel who arranged to aid the Yemenites called the project "Operation Magic Carpet."

Thirty-seven years later, in 1985, the Israelis did very much the same for the Ethiopian Jews. These black Jews, sometimes called *Falashas*, were starving and homeless, but the Ethiopian government did not want to let them go. The Israelis rescued them secretly, in airplanes which landed near the border of Ethiopia. This airlift was called "Operation Moses" in memory of another story in the Bible, which told how Moses led the Israelites out of Egypt into their promised land.

Jews are continually returning to Israel from different places. On May 14, 1948, the new country's Declaration of Independence promised that the Jewish nation would be open for the "ingathering of the exiles." That meant that it would be open to every Jew, anywhere in the world, who wanted to live there.

After World War II, thousands of sick and homeless Jewish refugees came to Israel. More recently, Soviet Jews who have been allowed to leave their native land have come to Israel to build a new life. Jews from Morocco and Algeria and other lands where they are

These Ethiopian immigrants, sometimes called Falashas, *were brought to Israel by an airlift known as "Operation Moses."*

not free come to Israel. In addition, Jews from free nations such as the United States, England, and Sweden go there because they believe Jews should live in a Jewish State.

Israel's Government

Today, Israel is growing and working hard at being a democracy. It has a parliamentary form of government, which includes a legislative, executive, and judicial branch. Israeli citizens are guaranteed equality before the law, and at the age of eighteen everyone can vote.

The legislative body in Israel is called the *Knesset*, an ancient word that means "assembly." About 2,500 years ago, this was the name used for the assembly led by two great leaders, Ezra and Nehemiah. Like the old representative body, the new Knesset also has 120 members. Each one is elected for four years.

Israel has many different political parties. When election day comes, citizens vote for the list of candidates put forth by the party of their choice. Then the party that receives the most votes chooses its own leader to be prime minister. The prime minister stays in office as long as his or her political party is in power.

Today, Israel has so many political factions, or groups, that its politics can be confusing. Some of these factions join together to form larger groups called coalitions. Since no single party has ever received a majority of the vote, Israel has always been ruled by a coalition.

In addition to promising a homeland for all Jews, Israel's Declaration of Independence invited the Arabs living in the country to share the land and live with them in peace. After Israel's independence many Arabs left, but others remained to live and work in the new nation.

One out of every six citizens of Israel is a non-Jew. He or she may be a Muslim or a Christian Arab, a

Muslim Arabs wait outside a mosque in Jerusalem for prayers to begin. Religious Muslims pray five times a day.

Druze, or a Samaritan. The Druze are an important group in Israel that have their own secret religion. The Samaritans practice a religion which has not changed since biblical times.

The Hebrews and the Bedouins

Israel is a country whose history spans thousands of years. So many peoples have either lived here or passed through that the land is of special interest to archeologists. Archeologists are scientists who study the artifacts, or objects, left from past human life and activity. They look for mounds of earth, called "tels," where ancient cities lie buried. By examining and studying the objects they find there, they can learn many things about how people once lived.

The archeologists who explore Israel's past have discovered interesting things about an ancient people who once dwelled in the desert. They were called Hebrews, and they came into the area that is now Israel about 4,000 years ago. The Hebrews lived in tents made of goatskin, and wandered from place to place in search of water and food for their flocks. They stored their oil and grain in handmade pottery jars.

This ancient way of living can still be seen in Israel today among a group called the Bedouins. Like their ancestors, some Bedouin Arabs still live in black goatskin tents with no running water or electricity. They travel over the deserts searching for grass and water for their goats and sheep.

The Israeli government has tried to help the Bedouins to improve their lives by giving them new apartments with modern kitchens and bathrooms. The apartment houses were built in a city called Beersheba, in the middle of the Negev Desert, close to where the Bedouins live. Some of these wandering people learned to live in the city and accepted this new way of life. A few even travel north to the big cities of Jerusalem or Tel Aviv, to work together with other Arabs and Jews. Others were not happy with modern life, and returned to the desert and their ancient way of living.

The Bedouins' way of life is not at all like that of the Arabs who live in villages or cities. These Arabs might be Christians or Muslims. They dwell in stone houses or apartment buildings, mostly among other Arabs. They may be farmers, shopkeepers, teachers, construction workers, or police officers. In Israel Arabs have their own schools, where children study in the Arabic language. Like many Westerners, they have televisions and cars, and the young people like to listen to rock music and drink Coca Cola.

Modern City Life

Most Israeli Jews live in cities, often in big apartment houses. Each apartment has a balcony where the family can sit and relax, eat supper on a warm night, and call down to their friends passing by on the street. These Israelis have radios and TVs, stereos, and sometimes even video games.

Religious Jews, who practice the traditional beliefs passed down for centuries, do not accept these modern amusements. They live in their own communities and

*In Jerusalem, religious Jews such as these Orthodox men and
boys walk to a synagogue before the Sabbath begins.*

wear special clothes that set them apart from the non-
religious Jews. The girls dress modestly, with long sleeves
and stockings covering their arms and legs. The boys do
not wear shorts, and always cover their heads with a
small, round hat called a *kippah*, or *yarmulka*.

Most of the Jewish children live at home with their
parents and go to a school nearby where they study in

Hebrew. Although Hebrew was once used only for prayer, today it has been made into a modern language. It has new words for things that did not exist in the Bible, such as "supermarket," "radar," and "computer."

Some Israeli families live in the smaller cities of the south—Beersheba, Dimona, or Eilat, the city at the southern tip of Israel on the Red Sea. Many others live in the central part of the country in larger cities such as Haifa, Tel Aviv, or Natanya.

These cities have tall office buildings, big hotels, and lots of traffic. Most industry is also centered in the cities. Although Israel does not have iron, coal, oil, or other important raw materials, its factories produce a wide variety of manufactured goods. Some products made in Israel are medical and telecommunications equipment and modern agricultural and irrigation machinery. Israelis have also developed new ideas in the fields of solar energy, computer hardware and software, and small arms defensive weapons.

An important scientific breakthrough in Israel could make a big difference to countries throughout the Middle East. Israeli scientists have developed efficient methods to remove the salt from seawater and use it for drinking. Today the country has several desalinization plants.

As a leader in cutting and polishing diamonds, Israel produces 80 percent of the world's output of these

Tel Aviv is a modern city with a number of skyscrapers. To the lower right in this view, Independence Garden overlooks the Mediterranean Sea.

precious stones. It also has a fashion industry which is known throughout the world.

The central squares of Israel's cities have many kinds of shops and restaurants. In the major cities, there is even a fast-food hamburger chain called Mc-David where you can buy American-style hamburgers and french fries.

The cities that are built along the Mediterranean Sea have beaches and parks, and outdoor cafes where you can watch the people go by while enjoying a cup of coffee or juice. In summertime a popular drink is *ice-café*, made with cold coffee, ice cream, fresh fruit, and whipped cream.

New Crops in the Desert

Outside the cities, Jews may live in *moshavim*, small villages where most of the people are farmers. Each *moshav* family has its own house and fields. Sometimes the farmers share important farm machinery. They may help each other with the work, but each one is independent.

Although Israel was once considered a desert land, all kinds of vegetables and fruits are grown here now. Oranges have been an important crop in this area for centuries. In recent times, Jewish pioneers planted more fruit trees. Today, orchards of orange, lemon, and grapefruit trees are a common sight in the Israeli countryside.

Olive trees also grow in Israel. In the fall, when the olives ripen, the farmers beat the olive trees until the fruit falls. Then they squeeze the olives in presses to make olive oil, or sell them to eat whole.

Israeli farmers have developed methods to grow apples and cherries, cotton, peanuts, and tomatoes. Most recently, they have experimented with unusual fruits such as kiwis, persimmons, and leechees. Now,

The bright green trees of a productive orchard rise from land that receives little rainfall. Israel is a world leader in desert agriculture.

using modern methods of irrigation, a great variety of crops can be grown here even though most areas receive no more than a small amount of rain in the winter and none at all in summer.

Life on a Kibbutz

Besides the moshav—the farm village—Jews may also live in a cooperative settlement called a *kibbutz*. In a kibbutz family members may not live together in the same house. Parents sometimes live in small cottages, while their children may live in a children's house as one giant family. Mothers and fathers work all morning and part of the afternoon while children go to school. After work the parents visit with their children, perhaps eat a meal with them, and tuck them into bed in the children's house.

Adults in a kibbutz might work in the fields, the orchards, the cow barns, the kitchen, or the kibbutz factory or office. A kibbutz may also have its own shoe-maker, clothing store, and a garage to fix its trucks, cars, and tractors.

Although life on the kibbutz is the same as city or village life in some ways, it is very different in others. The main difference is that all the people on the kibbutz decide together how to spend the money they earn, and they share equally everything the community has. This special life-style is found only in Israel, and even here, only a small part of the Jews are "kibbutznicks."

The Jewish Sabbath

Whether an Israeli lives in a kibbutz, a moshav, an Arab village, a big city, or a Bedouin camp, he or she will go to school or work for six days a week. These six days, though, are not the same for everyone. Muslim boys or girls may go to the mosque with their parents on

Near the city of Haifa in northern Israel, the buildings of the kibbutz Hanaton are surrounded by fertile fields.

Friday. For these Arab children, schools are closed on that day, and Arab stores are shut tight.

Just as the Muslim day of worship ends on Friday night, the Jewish Sabbath begins. All the stores close, the buses stop running, and the Jews have a break from work and school. Religious families may go to a synagogue, but others will head for the beaches, hike in the hills, or visit with friends.

When the third star appears in the sky on Saturday night, the Jewish Sabbath ends, and the Christian children of Israel prepare for their Sabbath on Sunday. It is their turn to close their shops and go to church while the busy Israeli life bustles around them.

Because people of many cultures live side by side, this new, small nation faces many problems. Neighboring Arab countries threaten Israel's security, and its people have learned to live with the threat of war. One of the first words an Israeli child learns is *Shalom*, which means "peace." People greet each other on the street with Shalom instead of hello. In the Arabic language, they say *Salaam*. For most of Israel's citizens, finding a way to live together in peace is a very important goal.

Early on Friday evenings, Jews begin to gather at the Kotel, *a small section of the wall that surrounded the ancient Temple of Jerusalem. Many Israelis and visitors come here to start the Sabbath, which begins on Friday at sunset.*

2. A Dream of Peace

Even though Israel is not much bigger than the state of New Jersey, it is a hotbed of political activity and the topic of much discussion. People question everything from its foreign policy, to the military and economic aid the United States provides for Israel. Most of the questions are complex, confusing, and still unsolved.

Israel's land is claimed by many. Three major religions—Judaism, Christianity, and Islam—consider Israel to be a holy place. Each group worships in its own synagogues, churches, or mosques. Many Jews live outside of Israel in different countries, watching Israeli affairs with interest and concern.

Jews who were born within Israel are called *sabras*. The sabra is the sweet but prickly fruit of the cactus plant that grows all over the country. Like the plant, the native Israeli Jews can be gruff or "prickly" on the surface, but are friendly or "sweet" inside.

Israelis are very concerned with what the world thinks about Jews, and Israel as a nation. Throughout their history the Jews have been oppressed, or abused, by other countries. Before Israel became a nation, Jews were not strong enough as a group to protect themselves. They often suffered at the hands of others, were treated harshly, and left with no place to go. Today, Israeli Jews are proud to have their own country with its own army. Jews from other nations worldwide are free to find new homes in Israel.

Hebrew is the main language of Israel. For many centuries, Jews who lived outside their land for thousands of years had stopped speaking Hebrew, except in traditional prayer. In Palestine Eliezer Ben-Yehudah devoted his life to bringing Hebrew back into the mainstream of the twentieth century. He wrote a Hebrew dictionary, creating new words for modern vocabulary needs. Though his neighbors spoke many different languages, he stubbornly fought to unify the people with one common language. Today, the government has special schools called *ulpans* where new immigrants can learn Hebrew quickly.

The Historic Bible

To understand Israel, it is important to understand its strong ties with its ancient past. This country must deal with many cultural differences and conflicts, even among Jewish citizens, but the Bible is a heritage its people all share. The stories of the Bible represent the common history and origins of Israel, as well as describing many places that still exist today. The cities of Jerusalem, Ashkelon, Jaffa, and Eilat were also major

This olive tree, located in the Garden of Gethsemane, is said to be 2,000 years old. It is believed that Jesus waited here for the Romans to arrest him.

cities in biblical times. The Dead Sea and the caves of Galilee, both mentioned in the Bible, are constant reminders to Israelis of their continuing link to the past.

Arabs, too, accept the history of the Bible. They may trace their own ancestry back to one of the ancient peoples who lived in the land we know as Israel. Most Muslim Arabs believe that the Arab people began with

Ishmael, the biblical character who was the oldest son of Abraham. Jews also trace their origin to Abraham and his family.

Biblical names for children are quite popular throughout Israel. Some common names for girls are Sarah, Rebecca, Rachel, and Deborah. Boys are often called Jacob, Joseph, David, Daniel, or even Israel.

The old Jewish system of dividing the year into months and weeks according to the moon comes from the Bible. However, Israelis also use a modern calendar that is based on the sun. The Jewish calendar counts the years dating from the time the ancient Hebrews once believed to be the creation of the world. By this system, the year 1987 is counted as the year 5748.

New Twists on Old Customs

Jewish holidays also date back thousands of years, and many are described in the Bible in great detail. Many of the ancient customs associated with the holidays are still practiced by the Jews of today's Israel.

The Bible often refers to group dancing. The ancient Israelites performed victory dances in the streets, and celebrated harvest festivals with dance as well. Young girls and boys met other people at dances at different times throughout the year. Wedding and religious dancing also were common to biblical times.

Today, old customs have found new life in a modern Israeli style of folk dancing. Jews brought dances to Israel from many different lands. From the Arabs came the *debka*, the line dance of men. Yemenite Jews also had their particular style of dance, which is now practiced by modern Israeli dance groups such as Inbal Dance Theatre and the Jerusalem Dance Company.

In parts of eastern Europe, Russia, Poland, and the Ukraine, the circle dance was common. It was adapted by the Jewish pioneers who came to what is now Israel in the beginning of the twentieth century. This dance is now known as the *hora*.

Among the *Hasidim*, a group of Jews who strictly observe the separation of the sexes, the men and women dance separately. If they come together, they each hold one end of the handkerchief so that their hands do not touch.

All of these different styles of dance are part of a new Israeli culture. Every Saturday evening, after the Jewish Sabbath has ended, Israelis of all ages join the folk dancing in central squares and local parks. Modern equipment enhances the biblical dancing customs with loudspeakers, and musical recordings. Dancing is a part of many celebrations, especially those that have to do with weddings and holidays.

The music of Israel, like its dances, is a combination of different styles, and has its roots in biblical tradition.

Israelis dance at the Wailing Wall in Jerusalem to celebrate holidays or important national events.

Each year Israelis hold a contest to see who can create the best song from the words of the traditional Jewish prayers. Many of the songs entered in the contest become popular songs on the radio. Since the final judging is televised, families watch the special program to discover which song will be number one.

Israel sends many of its singers and songs to Western Europe and America. Israelis won second place in 1979 and 1980 in the Eurovision Song Contest, a com-

Israeli boys and girls enjoy singing together during a youth group activity.

petition in which many European countries participate. Within Israel itself, there are many music festivals. Besides the world famous Israel Philharmonic Orchestra, which makes its home in Tel Aviv, the cities of Jerusalem, Haifa, Natanya, and Beersheba have their own orchestras.

Many of the popular songs about life in Israel are about love, war, and hopes for peace. Soldiers and other young people express their dream of a peaceful future through a song called "Next Year." "Wait and see, wait and see what a world it will be...next year." Another song, called "Tomorrow," ends with the words, "All this is not a dream; it's as certain as the sun at noontime...And if not tomorrow, then the day after."

Fighting for the Jewish Nation

The threat of war is never far from an Israeli's mind, as the battles rage in the Middle East. Israel has had to fight many wars against neighboring countries. Even more often it has been called upon to defend its borders against enemies of all kinds who would like to destroy the Jewish nation. These terrorists often try to sneak across the borders into Israel, throwing bombs, attacking buses, and killing people. For this reason, serving in the Israeli army is dangerous even when there is no war. Soldiers are often injured or killed.

The army occupies an important part of the life of Israeli Jews. Most young men and women must serve in the army for two years, and are drafted right after graduation from high school. Men must also serve one month each year until they reach the age of fifty-five. Some Jewish people with strong religious beliefs are excused from army service, and Israeli Arabs are not allowed to be soldiers. Israel is one of the few nations in the world that drafts women into its army.

Young women in the Israeli army rest on the campus of Tel Aviv University. Soldiers go on many trips throughout Israel.

Most Jewish families know at least one young person in the army. For this reason, and because of terrorist attacks, people listen closely for news about politics, battles, or border incidents. Israelis can hear news broadcasts on public buses. In times of trouble, important news is announced on loudspeakers in neighborhood parks.

Peace is a dream shared by all the people of Israel. Most citizens hope that eventually there will be more understanding among the different groups within their country. They look for ways to improve relations between Jews and Arabs, and between religious and non-religious Jews. They try to be hopeful in the face of constant problems. "If not tomorrow," they say, "then the day after."

3. An Old New Land

Israel's history began a very long time ago. Long before people knew how to write and keep written records, cave dwellers lived in the hills around the big lake which is now called the Sea of Galilee. Later they learned to plant seeds and grow their own food. Some of the world's first farmers cultivated the land more than 100,000 years ago.

Israel was one of the earliest centers of ancient civilization in the world. As a land bridge connecting the three continents of Africa, Europe, and Asia, this small country has always been a crossroads for traders.

A Land of Constant Change

The land that is now called Israel has had many conquerors and many names. The oldest recorded name for this area is Canaan. The Canaanites were farmers but they also built cities. Wandering on the same land were nomads who had no permanent homes. The nomads raised sheep and goats, and traveled in search of pasture land for their flocks.

About 3,200 years ago, the Canaanites were conquered by the Israelites. The Israelites, who may have

People have lived on the land around the Sea of Galilee for many thousands of years.

been nomads originally, then set up their own government. The Hebrew Bible tells the history of the Israelite tribes.

When the Israelites combined the area under one rule, they named it Israel. At this time, about the tenth century B.C.E. (before the birth of Christ and the beginning of our own calendar), the Israelites had strong kings. First there was King Saul, then King David, and his son Solomon, who ruled one nation. After Solomon's death, though, the nation divided into two parts. The northern part kept the name of Israel. The southern part, including the ancient capital of Jerusalem, was called Judah, after the tribe that ruled there. The word *Jew* comes from this name.

While the early Israelites lived in their land, other peoples came to settle there, too. Among them were the Phoenicians and the Philistines. They came east from the area around the Aegean Sea which is now Greece.

The Philistines often fought with the Israelites over the land. After many battles the Israelites defeated them, and the Philistines disappeared long ago. However, this ancient people later gave the land the name of Palestine, by which it was known until 1948.

Several hundred years after the Philistines, Assyria, a powerful new nation to the north, destroyed the northern kingdom of Israel. Only Judah was left as an independent country. Then Judah, too, was finally conquered by Babylonia in 587 B.C.E. Most of the Judeans were forced to leave their homeland and go to live in Babylonia. When Babylonia was defeated by Persia, the Persian rulers allowed the Israelites to return and rebuild their country.

Greeks and Romans

In 332 B.C.E., Alexander the Great, a famous general from Macedonia, now part of Greece, marched into the Middle East. He took over every country in the area, including tiny Judah.

Even after Alexander's death, the region remained under Greek rule for about three hundred years. During that time Judah managed to regain its independence after a war with Antiochus IV, the Greek king, who ruled from Syria. The fighters who led the army of Judah, the Maccabees, became the new kings of Judah for more than one hundred years.

But such a small nation, surrounded by great powers and strong armies, could not remain independent. The Romans, who lived in what is now Italy, formed the most powerful empire in the world. They took over the lands of the Middle East, including Judah. Judah was the only area of the ancient Israelite nation still occupied mainly by Jews.

At first the Romans allowed Judah some independence, but later they became harsh rulers. They had no patience with the Judeans, who insisted on practicing their own religion. Roman rulers became angry when groups of Jews constantly rebelled against Roman rule. Finally, in a bitter battle between the Roman army and the Jews, Jerusalem was burned, and all the inhabitants were forced to flee the city. This decisive battle took place in the year 70 C.E. (counting after the birth of Christ).

Although the Jews were badly beaten, they were not ready to give up. They established new communities and centers of study all over Judah and the north, and waited for a new leader. They hoped to regain their land, just as the Maccabees had done by fighting the Greeks.

This time, however, the Jews were not successful. Their leader, Simon Bar Kokhba, was defeated by the Romans. Rome now proclaimed that no Jew could live in the city of Jerusalem ever again. They changed the name of the area from Judea, the Latin name for Judah, to Palestine. The land became desolate. With no one to farm and plant, it gradually turned into a desert.

This second exile of the nation of Israel was to last almost 2,000 years. All that time Jews prayed for the return to their homeland. They longed for the city of Jerusalem, where the ancient Temple had first been built in the days of King Solomon.

Jews also had another name for the land of Israel and their holy city of Jerusalem. They called it *Tzee-yon* in Hebrew, or *Zion*. Later, the desire of the Jews to return to their old home, to rule their own nation as they once had, came to be called Zionism.

Zionism brought many Jews back to what was now Palestine. They came alone, just to see the "Holy Land," or in groups to settle in various cities of the area. Yet they never became strong enough to rule the land of their ancestors.

The Rise of Islam

In the beginning of the seventh century—more than 500 years after the burning of Jerusalem—a leader named Muhammad arose. He was from the city of Mecca in Arabia, a vast area of deserts and mountains not far from Palestine. Muhammad taught his people a new religion based on a belief in one God, known as *Allah*. The majority of Arabians accepted this new way of life, and Mecca became their most sacred city. Then, after Muhammad's death, his followers rode out of Arabia with an army of the faithful. They conquered Jerusalem and all of Palestine.

The army spread north to Syria, and south to Egypt and all of North Africa. Wherever Muhammad's followers conquered, the people adopted his new religion. First known as Muhammadanism, later it was called Islam, or the Muslim religion.

Muslims spread the culture and language of Arabia throughout the Middle East. Those who accepted the

After Palestine was conquered by the Muslims, the Arab rulers directed the building of mosques. The Mosque of Omar in Jerusalem, also called the Dome of the Rock, has a beautiful gold-plated dome.

new religion and culture came to be called Arabs. They were loyal to the powerful Arab leaders who ruled Palestine and the area around it.

When Muslims first began to conquer and control the lands of the East, Europe was weak and divided. By the year 1085, though, Europe was stronger. When the Christian church called for a crusade against Muslim rule in Palestine, many people answered the call. Armies from France, England, and Germany marched through all of Europe, captured Jerusalem, and established Christian rule in parts of Palestine. Some European Christians stayed and settled there at this time. They lived among Arabic-speaking Muslims and Jews.

The Christian kingdom in the Holy Land did not last very long. A new leader, Saladin, united all the Arabs behind him and drove the Christians out in 1291.

While one invader after another conquered and ruled, many things remained the same. Nomads still wandered through the land, much of it desert by now, in search of water and green pastures for their flocks. Arab peasants, the *fellahin*, continued to farm the land and to live in small villages. Jews, too, established permanent homes in centers of Jewish learning such as Safed, Tiberius, and Jerusalem. Others came just to see the Holy Land once before they died. Some even waited there to die so they could be buried in the holy ground of Jerusalem.

After Saladin, the Turkish Ottoman Empire ruled for four hundred years. It controlled almost all of the Middle East, Turkey, and parts of southeastern Europe.

Israel's Early Heroes

Under Turkish rule, a new kind of Jew began coming from Europe into Palestine. These Jews wanted to rebuild Zion, the old Jewish nation. Young and idealistic, they bought land that the Arab landlords had considered worthless. They farmed deserts, drained swamplands, brought in modern methods of agriculture, and started Jewish settlements. To protect themselves, they posted Jewish guards around their communities.

Over time, this group of young men and women, mostly from Eastern Europe, changed the land of Israel. From a poor and desolate area, it became a territory with new cities, settlements, and roads. The Zionists believed in their right to reclaim their homeland. According to the Bible, the land was promised to them by God. They were ready to work to fulfill their dream.

Theodore Herzl was a Jewish journalist from Vienna. In the late nineteenth century, he helped build the Zionist dream for many European Jews. He believed that the only way to stop anti-Semitism—hatred of Jews because of their religion and/or nationality—was to allow the Jews to live in their own country.

Herzl wrote a book, *The Old-New Land*, which described his idea of what a Jewish homeland would be like. Then in 1897, he organized the first world meeting of Zionists. Delegates to this meeting began to make plans for a Jewish nation. Herzl also visited many important people in Europe to try to gain their support.

Although he did not live to see the birth of modern Israel, Herzl never stopped working for it. His motto was: "If you will it, it is no dream." By that he meant that if people want something badly enough, it can happen.

Theodore Herzl was not the only one working hard to create a new Jewish nation. Chaim (pronounced Hayim) Weizmann was another of Israel's early heroes. Weizmann was a Russian Jew and a devoted Zionist. After studying biochemistry in Germany and Switzerland, he moved to England. There he worked as a teacher and scientist at the University of Manchester.

During World War I, Chaim Weizmann helped the British win the war by inventing acetone. That important new material was used for manufacturing many types of weapons. Through this discovery, and his work in defense, Weizmann met many of the top officials in the British government and convinced them to support the Zionist cause. The result of this important achievement was the Balfour Declaration. It was named after the Englishman, Lord Arthur James Balfour, who was then the British foreign secretary. The declaration said

Theodore Herzl (left) *was a leader of the early Zionist movement.*
Chaim Weizmann (right), *a Russian Jew who moved to England,*
helped gain British support for a Jewish homeland.

that England "looked favorably" on the creation of a
Jewish homeland in Palestine.

The Balfour Declaration was a great victory for
the Jews. At last a major country such as England was
ready to support their goal. As a result, many more Jews
settled in Palestine. Later, when the English and other
Allied forces won World War I, the British seized a
large part of the Middle East, including Palestine, from
the Turks.

Palestine's Door Closes

During the 1930s, still more Jews came to Palestine. By that time, though, England had begun to change its mind about a Jewish homeland. The Arabs urged the British not to allow any more Jews to enter Palestine. They were afraid that they would lose their own influence in the Middle East if too many Jewish settlers came.

The Arabs lived in and ruled many Middle Eastern countries. In 1922 the land of TransJordan had been created by the British from the eastern part of Palestine. That nation, too, was governed by Arabs. Many Arab leaders ruled in countries which sold petroleum to England. Because England needed this oil, its government tried to please these leaders by stopping almost all Jewish immigration to Palestine, while allowing Arab immigrants to continue coming in.

The British closed the door of Palestine at a very bad time. In the period before and during World War II, the Nazis in Germany threatened and later killed millions of Jews living in Europe. Many tried to leave but had no place to go. Almost none of the countries of Europe and North or South America wanted any new immigrants. As a result, many Jews who might have been saved were murdered by the Nazis in wartime

David Ben-Gurion was an important leader of the Jewish community in Palestine and became the prime minister of the new nation of Israel.

concentration camps. This terrible, tragic event came to be known as the Holocaust.

In 1945, after the horrors of World War II had ended, the Jews realized that six million of their people had been killed. They were more determined than ever to create a country of their own. And now, at last, shocked by what had happened in the war, other nations were ready to help.

A Jewish Pioneer

Many Jews inside Palestine played important roles in creating the Jewish homeland. The work of establishing the new nation involved hundreds of dedicated men and women, and many more hundreds of new ideas. In the early years of planning, one of the Jewish pioneers who worked hardest for this goal was David Ben-Gurion.

Ben-Gurion was born in Russia in 1886, but settled in Palestine when he was just twenty years old. He believed that every Jew must go to live in the ancient homeland. In 1917, when the Balfour Declaration was signed, Ben-Gurion was in the United States. He helped form youth organizations to encourage young American Jews to settle in Palestine.

Eventually becoming one of the most important leaders of the Jewish community in Palestine, Ben-Gurion worked hard to unite the many Jewish factions, or groups, into one government. He led the opposition against the British when they tried to stop immigration of Jews into Palestine. During World War II, he supported England because it fought against Nazi Germany.

Ben-Gurion helped form a Jewish brigade, made up of Jewish soldiers from Palestine, which went to fight the Nazis in Europe. Jews had often served as soldiers for other nations. However, this was the first time since the destruction of Jerusalem in 70 C.E. that they had fought as soldiers under their own flag.

The New Nation

In 1947, when the United Nations voted to create a new Jewish nation, the Jews were ready with a plan for their own army and their own government. They were eager to establish self-rule, and could hardly wait to begin.

The vote in the United Nations General Assembly in New York was broadcast throughout Palestine. On Allenby Street, the main street of the city of Tel Aviv, a big board had been erected. On it were the names of all the nations that would vote at the United Nations. As each nation cast its vote, yes or no, it was placed on the board for all to see. Large crowds stood by to watch and count. It was very quiet as everyone waited.

When there were at last enough "yes" votes to carry the resolution, the crowd began shouting for joy. They hugged and kissed each other on the street, dancing and singing and crying. At last, after almost 2,000 years of waiting, the Jewish people again had a homeland.

Under the United Nations partition plan, Israel's borders covered less territory than they do today, and included only half of the city of Jerusalem. The land had been divided to allow for a new Palestinian country for the Arabs. Although Israel would be very small, the Jews were happy to have even part of their ancient homeland.

On May 14, 1948, the day the British officially left Palestine, the Jewish leaders gathered in a room of the Tel Aviv Museum to declare to the world that they were a nation. From then on, their land would be called Israel. David Ben-Gurion read the declaration, and it was heard over the radio by citizens throughout the new country. Those who lived near enough, assembled outside the museum to wait for Ben-Gurion to make his announcement. When it came, there was more celebrating.

It seemed as if every Jewish man, woman, and child in the new land of Israel was rejoicing. Even some of Israel's Arab citizens were happy for the Jews. Others were angry and were determined to continue fighting against the new nation.

The War of Independence

The day after the British soldiers left, the Arab countries of Egypt, Iraq, Jordan, Lebanon, Syria, and a group from Saudi Arabia invaded Israel. Israel's army had hardly been organized, but the soldiers had no choice. They had to fight.

The war continued for about one year. Finally, in July 1949, the countries signed separate agreements that ended the fighting.

When the war—called the War of Independence by Israel—was finally over, the Jewish nation had won more territory than it had originally been granted. During that year much had happened within Israel itself. The new nation now had an army, a declaration of independence, and a complete government. It was recognized by most of the nations of the world, including the Soviet Union and the United States. The head of the new government, the prime minister, was David Ben-Gurion. Its first president was Chaim Weizmann.

A Nation at War

Since its War of Independence, Israel has continually been forced to defend itself against attacks from Arabs who did not want a Jewish nation in the Middle East. In 1956, Egypt started a blockade. Egyptian forces had already blocked Israeli passage through the Suez Canal for some time. Now they succeeded in preventing Israel's ships from passing through the straits of Tiran into the Red Sea and reaching the port of Eilat.

To protect its right to freedom of the seas, Israel had to fight back. With the help of France and England, it moved against Egyptian bases in the Sinai Desert and

The fighting that followed Israel's independence ended with a truce between the Israelis and neighboring Arab countries. Here Moshe Dayan meets with Colonel Abdullah el Tel in No-Man's Land, Jerusalem, on March 6, 1949.

succeeded in reaching the Suez Canal. The United States helped persuade Egypt to allow Israel free access to the Red Sea and the Canal. Israel, in exchange, returned all the captured territory to Egypt.

The second major action between Israel and other Arab states took place in 1967. This time Egypt, Jordan, and Syria prepared to attack Israel. In spite of having to fight on three of its borders at once, the Israeli armed forces managed a stunning victory in only six days.

In the south, they destroyed the Egyptian air force while it was still on the ground, and again took control of the Sinai Desert. Then, turning to the west, they drove the Jordanian army out of east Jerusalem and united the city under Jewish rule for the first time in thousands of years. Israeli forces also managed to drive back Syria's army and capture the Golan Heights, bordering Israel in the north.

In the 1967 war, known as "The Six-Day War," Israel conquered land on the west bank of the Jordan River. This area is referred to in the Bible as Judah and Samaria. Most other people call it "the West Bank," or—along with the Gaza Strip, a small piece of land near Egypt—the "occupied" or "administered" territories.

Many Palestinians have lived on the West Bank for generations. Others fled there as refugees during Israel's War of Independence. This was the land that had been set aside as the Palestinian Arab nation in the United Nations partition plan. Jews, too, had once lived here until Arab attacks drove them away.

When the United Nations first suggested partition, Palestinians refused to accept a small area for their own country. They insisted on having the entire territory and refused to set up a government. As a result, the West Bank was taken over by the Jordanians. It was ruled as part of Jordan from 1948 until 1967, when it was occupied by Israel.

When Israel took over the West Bank, many Palestinian refugees were still living in temporary camps. Some of these people had settled in other Arab lands. Most are still without citizenship in any country.

In October 1973, Egypt and Syria once again attempted to destroy Israel. On *Yom Kippur*, the holiest day of the Jewish year, their armies invaded on two fronts, taking the Israelis by surprise. The Israel Defense Force had to call its soldiers out of the synagogues to defend the country against the Arab armies.

Israel's army managed to drive back the attackers, but suffered heavy losses. After two weeks of fighting, a cease-fire was arranged with the help of the United States.

After the Yom Kippur War, Palestinians became more active on their own behalf instead of depending on other countries to help them. Their organization, the Palestine Liberation Organization, or PLO, became a kind of government in exile. Members of this group have devoted their lives to overcoming Israel and driving out the Jews. Although other Palestinians have tried to make peace, they have not succeeded.

Making Peace With Egypt

Among all of Israel's neighbors, Egypt is the only country that made peace with the Jewish nation. In

During the 1973 Yom Kippur War, Israeli soldiers pray in their trenches near the battle lines.

November 1977, Egyptian President Anwar Sadat came to Jerusalem to meet with Menachem Begin, who was then Israel's prime minister. This was the first time that an Arab leader had ever agreed to come to Israel. Until that time, all the Arab nations had refused to recognize its existence.

Sadat's visit was a remarkable event for both countries. It led to further meetings, including the famous Camp David agreements in September 1978. The final Israel-Egypt Peace Treaty was signed in Washington, D.C., on March 26, 1979. U.S. President Jimmy Carter, who had helped bring the two leaders together, witnessed this historic event.

In the peace treaty, Israel and Egypt agreed to have normal relations. They pledged to set up embassies in each other's capitals, establish political and trade relations, and exchange visits of government officials. In return for Egypt's promise not to fight against Israel, Israel agreed to return the Sinai Desert land that it had conquered in 1967.

Sadat's and Begin's efforts toward peace led to a Nobel Peace Prize for the two leaders. Both hoped that the Israel-Egypt Peace Treaty would encourage other Arab nations to make peace. However, this is not what happened. Instead, Arab governments and leaders refused to have anything to do with Egypt and accused Sadat of giving in to Israel.

In 1979 at Camp David, Maryland, Israel's Prime Minister Menachem Begin (right), *Egyptian President Anwar Sadat* (left), *and U.S. President Jimmy Carter* (center) *sign an Israeli-Egyptian peace treaty.*

The Palestinian Liberation Army

Extreme groups in Arab countries renewed their efforts to destroy Israel, including sending men, money, and arms to the Palestine Liberation Organization.

PLO leaders looked for a safe place to establish themselves. At the beginning of its existence, the PLO operated out of Jordan and Egypt. But the Jordanians did not like or trust the Palestinian guerrilla fighters. Jordan's King Hussein felt they were trying to control his government.

In September 1970, King Hussein drove the PLO and all its followers out of Jordan. Later in the 1970s, Egypt's peace treaty with Israel made PLO activity unacceptable there, too. The Palestine Liberation Army began to settle in Lebanon, and gradually more people joined them. These supporters included not only Palestinians, but many other Arabs who wanted to destroy Israel and create their own government.

The civil war in Lebanon between Christian and Muslim groups resulted in a weak Lebanese government that could not control PLO activities. As a result, PLO attacks against the northern border of Israel increased. In addition, terrorists, trained and organized in southern Lebanon, were sent all over the world. They planted bombs, hijacked airplanes, and kidnapped citizens of other countries as well as Israel. Their goal, they claimed, was to make the world aware of the injustice done to the Palestinian people. They vowed to continue fighting until they got their own homeland.

War In Lebanon

Finally, in 1982, after continued attacks of this kind, as well as constant shelling of the Jewish settlements in the northern Galilee, Israel decided to act. Its soldiers marched across the Lebanese border and attacked the PLO strongholds in Lebanon.

This attack, called by Israel "Operation Peace for Galilee," was first planned as a small-scale operation. Its goal was to stop the Palestinian army from shooting at Israeli citizens from across the border.

The simple "operation" rapidly became a serious and drawn-out war which lasted much longer than expected. The Lebanese government had been weakened by the complicated civil war which had been going on in Lebanon for years before the Israeli attack. Because the Lebanese government had little power, Israel feared that if it withdrew its forces, the PLO would come right back.

Some of Israel's generals decided to advance toward Beirut, Lebanon's capital. These military leaders believed that by reaching Beirut, they could control the outcome of the civil war. Then they could help create a new government that would make peace with Israel.

The Israeli army occupied most of Lebanon for a short time. They soon found, however, that it was impossible to keep control over Lebanon's warring groups. The Israelis had some support from Lebanese Christian groups. However, the Muslims, backed by Syria, were violently opposed to the presence of Israel's army. The Lebanese Druze also fought against Israel. In addition to fighting the Israelis, each of these groups fought against the others.

Israel's friendship and sympathy for the Christian Arabs made some Israelis feel they should remain in Lebanon to help the Christians gain control of the government. Lebanese Christians had lived in peace with Israel for many years. The border they shared used to be known as "the good fence." Israel wanted to make it into a quiet border again.

As the months passed, remaining as an occupying force in Lebanon became too dangerous. Israeli soldiers were attacked by the different Lebanese armies, and criticized by the world.

Israel did succeed in destroying the Palestinian positions in southern Lebanon, and in making its border safer. It did not succeed in making peace with Lebanon. After more than a year, the Israel Defense Force pulled out, leaving the Lebanese fighting among themselves. Only a small force of Israeli soldiers remains in southern Lebanon to control the border.

Some people in other countries believe that this war should not have continued once its original goal was achieved. But more importantly, many of Israel's own citizens opposed the war. They felt their government was not doing the right thing.

Pressure on the government eventually forced a new election in Israel on July 23, 1984. Prime Minister

Menachem Begin, the man who had been praised for making peace with Egypt, was now blamed for the war in Lebanon in which so many young Israeli soldiers had been killed and wounded. Begin retired, and a new leader, Yitzhak Shamir, now headed the *Likud* party.

Modern Political Issues

Within Israel today, the people still disagree about their country's role in the Lebanese war. Israelis also argue about many other issues, both in the Knesset and among themselves. One of these is how to manage the economy. With so much of the budget going to defense, Israel has less money available for social and economic programs.

The issues in the last election centered around the nation's economy. The Likud believes the government should have less control over economic policy. The Labor coalition, called *Ma-arakh*, wants more government control of the economy to help reduce increases in prices.

In the 1984 election, none of the political parties won a majority of the vote. It was impossible to create a new government without the two major parties, Likud and Labor, joining together. The coalition they formed was based on a very unusual kind of agreement. The head of Labor, Shimon Peres, headed the government

After the 1984 elections, Shimon Peres headed Israel's government for two years.

as prime minister, while the new head of Likud, Yitzhak Shamir, became the foreign minister. After two years, they exchanged jobs.

Because of the split vote in the two major coalitions, both Likud and Labor must take into consideration the demands of the smaller religious parties. If they do not, these small groups may decide not to support the government. That action would upset the current fragile balance of power. Today this political problem adds to the growing tension between religious and non-religious Jews.

Another issue of major concern to Israel's citizens is their country's relationship with the United States. Since their nation was formed in 1948, Israel has received American financial and military support. As the only democracy in the Middle East, it is an important U.S. ally.

All this American aid leads to disagreements within Israel itself. Some Israelis believe that a strong tie with America is their only hope of survival against so many enemies. Others say that relying on U.S. aid makes their country less than fully independent in its actions. In spite of differences of opinion on this issue, Israelis continue to feel very close to America and Americans. The two armies often work together and share military information.

Among the most pressing problems that Israel faces are how to encourage peace, and what to do with the West Bank. Some Israeli Jews would like to make it a part of the Jewish nation. Many have even gone to settle there, establishing new Jewish towns next to the old Arab villages. Another group wants to give the West Bank to the Palestine Liberation Organization so the Palestinians can have a land of their own. They say that peace is more important than territory. Still others claim the PLO is a terrorist group which will continue

A young Israeli guards a Jewish settlement. Both in the past and today, Jewish settlements near border areas face many dangers.

trying to destroy Israel. These Jews would like the Arabs in the West Bank to set up a different political organization with new leaders who promise to accept Israel.

Israeli Arabs also disagree about what to do. Many consider the PLO to be the government of Palestine and would like it to be recognized. They see Israel as a strong nation which has nothing to fear from Arab enemies. Other Arabs believe that once Palestinians have a land of their own, they will not have to fight against Israel. Still other groups, both in Israel itself and on the West Bank, would like to set up a different organization. They want to elect leaders who are willing to live in peace with the Jews.

Unless the Israelis and Arabs can solve these urgent problems, the Middle East will continue to have wars, in spite of everyone's desire for peace. Israel and its Arab neighbors have been fighting for the past forty years. And yet, many people believe that peace is still possible if courageous leaders come forward to show their citizens the way.

4. *Everything Will Be Okay*

One of the most common words in an Israeli's vocabulary is *b'seder*. The word *seder* really means "order," and with the *b'* in front, it means "in order." However, it also has the exact same meaning as our word *okay*. The citizens of Israel always hope for the best, and even when there is trouble, Israelis assure each other: *"ha-kol b'seder"*—"Everything is okay."

"La-asot hayyim" is an interesting modern-day saying, too. It translates as "to make, or to do, life." But what an Israeli means by "la-asot hayyim" is "to live it up," or "to have a good time."

When someone does something special, Israelis say *"kol ha-kavod."* This expression is difficult to translate exactly, but it means "all honor to him/her," or "with all due respect." An Israeli may say "kol ha-kavod" about the late Egyptian President, Anwar Sadat, because he was the first leader of an Arab nation to come to Jerusalem and make peace with Israel.

Stories of the Bible

These are just a few of the more modern expressions used in Israel. The Jews also use some very old

Egypt's Anwar Sadat arrives in Jerusalem for peace talks with Israel's Menachem Begin.

sayings that come from the Bible or from the Talmud.

The Hebrew language uses the Bible as the basis for its grammar and vocabulary. Much of the Hebrew Bible is made up of separate books which contain wonderful stories about how the Jewish people began. Christians call this part of the Bible the Old Testament.

A popular tale from the Bible describes how Moses led the Israelites out of Egypt, across the Red Sea. After forty years of wandering in the desert, they finally came back to the "promised land." This land had been first promised to Abraham, Jacob's grandfather, and it is the same land that is called Israel today.

A favorite story among many Israelis tells about the deeds of the great King David, who ruled the ancient kingdom of Israel. One of the best-loved legends of King David is a story about his childhood. It was a time when Judah and Israel were at war with the Philistines. Young David was sent to the battlefield by his father to bring provisions to his older brothers who were in the army.

When he arrived, David found the soldiers excited and worried. The Philistines had brought a giant named Goliath to the front lines. Goliath dared any of the Israelites to fight against him. Whoever won this single combat would gain victory for his people.

Hearing the challenge, David volunteered to battle the giant, trusting in God and in his ability to defeat Goliath. David approached the front where Goliath stood and waited. When he was near enough to hear the giant's laughter, he calmly placed a stone in his slingshot, spun it around, and let fly. The stone struck exactly the right spot in the middle of Goliath's head. Fatally wounded, the giant fell down, and Israel and Judah were saved from the Philistines.

David's victory over Goliath made him a hero to his people. Later, he was chosen by the prophet Samuel to

The Tower of David, one of Jerusalem's landmarks, rises near the walls of the Old City.

be king. Throughout his life he proved to be a great warrior and leader.

Some religious people of all faiths believe that the Bible is the word of God and is absolutely true. Others recognize it as part truth and part legend. Regardless of their beliefs, all of them appreciate the stories in the Bible. These stories remain interesting and exciting, even though they are very old.

Wisdom of the Talmud

Besides the Bible, many Jews consider the Talmud to be an important part of their culture. The Talmud is not one, but a large number of books compiled by wise Jewish men. It was written during a 300-year period about 1,500 to 1,800 years ago. The books of the Talmud contain many different opinions about Jewish law and tradition. They also have lots of stories and wise sayings that are still popular today.

"If I am not for myself, who will be for me?" asked Hillel, a sage of the Talmud. Then he went on to ask: "But if I am *only* for myself, what am I?" Further, he says: "If not now, when?" These three questions, taken together, can be stated in the following way: First, we must help ourselves and take care of our needs. Then we must help others. And we must not postpone doing these things, because time is important.

Another saying that has been accepted among Jews in Israel is "All Israel is responsible one to another." This idea goes back to a time long before the country of Israel existed. Jews, even when they had no land of their own, usually considered themselves a nation. They believed that each Jew should help other Jews, with money or in other ways. This belief has led to a strong tradition of charity.

A Rich Yiddish Heritage

Besides traditional Hebrew expressions, some Israelis have sayings that come from the Yiddish heritage. Yiddish is a language that combines old German and Hebrew. It also includes a sprinkling of many languages from other European lands, and is written in the Hebrew alphabet. Jews who originated in Eastern Europe speak Yiddish, and have brought all its colorful expressions with them to Israel. When we hear them in English, they sound funny, but they are expressive, too. "Don't knock on my teakettle" is a Yiddish saying that means "Stop bothering me." If you want to say that something does not fit at all, or is not suitable, you might use the Yiddish expression: "It fits like a crown fits on a pig." "It will happen when hair grows on my palm," means it will never happen. If a child cannot sit still, or is very restless, a Yiddish-speaking person might say: "He has pins and needles."

Yiddish-speaking people have also contributed some wonderful legends to Israeli culture. Among everyone's favorites are the stories about Chelm.

Chelm is a make-believe town where everyone is very foolish. Once upon a time, according to Yiddish legend, an angel was delivering souls throughout the country. In his left hand he carried a collection of foolish souls, and in his right he held the wise souls. Just as he was flying over Chelm, he became distracted and by mistake dropped all the foolish souls at once. They all landed in the town of Chelm. That is why, when the people of Chelm meet to solve problems, they get some very strange results.

One story about the people of Chelm tells how they bought a cow who gave gold instead of milk; at least that is what they thought. It all began when some of the people of the town came upon a man sleeping by the side of the road. Near the man was his cow, and on the ground were some gold pieces that had fallen from the traveler's pocket.

After much thought, these foolish townspeople concluded that this gold must have come from the cow. They bought the cow from the astonished man, hoping to become rich with gold. Of course, the cow only gave milk, but the townspeople never did figure out why the cow stopped giving gold.

Along with Yiddish stories, Yiddish words are also heard in Israel. Young people who speak Hebrew may use them without even knowing that they are speaking another language.

One such word is *balagan.* In English, this word might be expressed as "total confusion." A student may come home after the first day of school and complain that it was a big balagan; no one knew where to go or what to do. A mother might say to her child: "You'd better clean up your room. It's a complete *balagan*." If she wants her child to hurry and do it right away, she will add the words *"chick-chock."* This is a slang expression for "hurry up," or "right this minute."

Another Yiddish expression that many children in Israel are familiar with is *"Oy-va-voy."* This is very hard to translate into English, but it means something like "Oh my!" or "Better watch out!" If a parent is particularly angry with something a child has done, he or she might warn: "Oy-va-voy to you!" meaning "You're going to get it! or "Better keep out of my way!"

Arab Stories and Legends

Arabic words have also come into Hebrew, and are part of the new Hebrew slang. One Arabic word often used by Hebrew-speaking Israelis is *yallah*. This word really means "giddyap" and was originally used to hurry along a horse or a donkey. Today, an Israeli caught in a traffic jam will be sure to hear one or more drivers shouting "Yallah!"

As the second language of Israel, Arabic is spoken by many Jews who came from the Middle East, as well as by Arabs. Although it is similar to the Hebrew language in many ways, and certain words are almost the same, it uses a different alphabet than Hebrew.

Arabs have their own stories and legends. Many of them come from the Koran, the Muslim holy book. One of these stories tells about Muhammad, the great prophet of Islam. Many Muslims believe that he wrote the Koran. According to the story, the angel Gabriel came to him each night and told him all the holy laws and stories.

One night, Muhammad dreamed of Jerusalem. In his dream, angels came and brought him to Mount Moriah, a holy mountain in the city, and then through the seven heavens. Mount Moriah was the place where the Jews had built their Temple to God in the years before Israel was exiled. When he woke the next morning, Muhammad discovered that he really had been to Jerusalem and back during the night.

To remember that miracle, the Arabs later built a beautiful mosque on the spot. It is called the *Al Aksa* mosque, which means the mosque of the far place.

New Stories in an Old Land

Although modern Israel is a new country, it is developing legends and stories very quickly. Some of these tell about the brave deeds of the pioneers who first came to settle in Israel in the early 1900s. Others are stories about soldiers who defended their own settlements against the invading Arab armies.

Sometimes, stories tell about Arabs and Jews helping each other instead of fighting each other. One especially hopeful story is about the Arab village of Iksal, which is in the Galilee in northern Israel. The people in this town were peaceful and kind and lived happily with their Jewish neighbors at a nearby kibbutz.

After Israel became independent, other Arabs came to attack this village, warning the people that they must help fight against the Jews, or else leave their homes. The Arabs of Iksal went to their friends at the kibbutz for help, and the Jews sent guards to protect the village. Because of this, Iksal was able to remain safe, and the people there are still loyal citizens of Israel. What happened at Iksal is a good example of the Arab proverb: "If I see to it that things are good for my neighbor, they'll be good for me, too."

In modern day Israel, stories like this one are still rare, but they are increasing. *"Al tidag,"* an Israeli might say, *"ha-kol yihyeh b'seder."* "Don't worry. Everything will be okay."

5. Happy Holidays!

Israel is a land of many holidays. In almost every month someone is celebrating a feast day or a fast day. Each religious group in Israel celebrates its own holidays. Israeli Jews share their festivals and holy days with Jews all over the world. Muslim Israelis celebrate just as their brothers and sisters do in other countries, while Christians have the same holidays as Christians do everywhere.

As a matter of fact, Israelis do not yet have a single official calendar. There is the Jewish calendar, the Muslim calendar, and several kinds of Christian calendars. Recently, Interns for Peace, an organization dedicated to helping Arabs and Jews learn more about each other, planned and published a complete calendar showing all the many special holidays. However, it is not yet widely used in Israel.

Because Israel is officially a Jewish nation, and most of its people are Jews, Jewish holidays are the most well known and most widely celebrated. The Orthodox, or the most observant Jews, emphasize prayer and attendance at synagogue for holidays. The less observant Jews see them as national celebrations and look for other ways to celebrate them.

The High Holidays

Jewish holidays may be divided into three different groups. The first group is the High Holidays, serious celebrations which Jews were commanded to observe from biblical times. They include *Rosh Hashanah* (the New Year), and *Yom Kippur* (the Day of Atonement). They usually fall in mid or late September, according to our calendar.

On these holidays, just as on the Sabbath, working is not allowed. Today in Israel, almost all Jewish stores and places of business are closed for both the New Year's holiday and Yom Kippur.

During Rosh Hashanah, celebrated for two days, religious Jews go to synagogue for long prayer services. Everyone dresses in his or her best clothes, usually something new for the New Year. Children often receive gifts for the holiday season. The less observant Jews use Rosh Hashanah as a time for family gatherings, or for outings in the warm, dry September weather. Beaches and parks are crowded, and there are often traffic jams.

Yom Kippur, which comes ten days after the New Year, is an especially solemn day. Jews atone for all their sins by fasting, or not eating, for the twenty-four hours of the holiday. Even those who are not at all religious may go to a synagogue on Yom Kippur. The Jewish television stations do not broadcast, and the streets are quiet, with no buses or cars to be seen anywhere.

The Pilgrim Festivals

The second type of Jewish holiday is the pilgrim festival. Pilgrim festivals are holidays that celebrate harvest times. The Bible directed Jews to make a pilgrimage to the Temple in Jerusalem on *Pesach* (Passover), *Sukkot* (the festival of booths), and *Shavuot* (the festival of weeks). Although the ancient Temple in Jerusalem no longer exists, and the method of celebration has changed, these festivals are still called by the same names.

Perhaps the most widely observed of all the Jewish holidays is Pesach, Passover, celebrated for a full week in March or April of the Western calendar. This festival recalls the biblical story of Moses. Moses led the children of Israel out of Egypt, where they had been slaves, and into the "Promised Land" of Israel.

Passover celebrates the first freedom and independence of the Jewish people, as well as the first harvest of springtime. One of the ways Jews remember these events is by eating a special kind of unleavened bread (bread which is not made with yeast and does not rise) called *matza*. Observant Jews will not eat bread or other foods made with yeast for a full week.

The center of the Passover celebration is the *seder*, the special meal on the first night of the holiday. During the seder, adults tell the story of Moses and the *exodus*, or going out, from Egypt.

Children play a very special role in the seder. The youngest children ask the adults four questions about the holiday. Then the adults at the table answer the questions by telling the many stories and legends associated with this most ancient of Jewish festivals.

During the retelling of these stories, a small piece of matza, called the *afikomen* (a Greek word meaning dessert), is broken in two, and one piece is hidden. The children find the missing piece and hide it from the grown-ups. Since the meal cannot be completed without this little piece of matza, the children usually get a present or a promise of money to persuade them to return the afikomen. This custom is the most fun for the young children, and it helps keep them awake throughout the long meal.

The holiday of Sukkot, although it occurs in September or October, right after the High Holidays, is also associated with Passover. Sukkot means booths or huts. The name refers to the little booths that many Jews build at this time of year to celebrate events and customs of long ago. When the ancient Israelites escaped from Egypt, they had no permanent homes and lived in booths like these. Also, at harvest time farmers often

Most Passover seders *include two or three generations of a family. Here* saba, *the grandfather, breaks up the tradition-al* matza.

built temporary shelters out in the fields while they were gathering the crops.

During Sukkot, if you go into a neighborhood in Israel where Orthodox Jews live, you will see many little booths standing in back yards or gardens or set up on the terraces of apartments. On the outside, each booth appears simple and bare, but the inside is usually decorated with beautiful fruits, flowers, and leaves. It may also have brightly colored posters on the walls.

Near or in the booth, or *sukkah*, is a small bundle of four different kinds of tree branches. This is called a *lulav*, and it is a symbol for the four types of trees grown in Israel. With it is a beautiful and sweet-smelling fruit that looks like a large lemon. It is called a citron in English, and in Hebrew *etrog*. These fruits of the harvest are carried to the synagogue during the week of Sukkot. In the sukkah, special blessings are recited over the lulav and the etrog, and the Jews pray for a good harvest.

The week of Sukkot ends with a big celebration called *Simhat Torah*, which means "the joy of the Law." It marks the day of the year when observant Jews finish reading the first five books of the Bible, known as the *Torah*. The reading takes place each week in the synagogue, and it takes a full year to read all five books. After Simhat Torah, religious Jews start to read again from the beginning.

On this day, Orthodox men carry the beautifully decorated scrolls of the Torah out of the synagogues. They dance and sing songs about the greatness of Jewish Law. The children follow them, singing and dancing down the streets. For those who do not go to synagogue, there are public celebrations in the parks with singing and dancing lasting late into the night.

The last of the three pilgrimage festivals is Shavuot. It takes place in late spring, exactly seven weeks after Passover. That is why it is called Shavuot ("Weeks"). The *bikurim* festival, the harvest of spring, marks the time when farmers used to bring the first fruits up to the Temple in Jerusalem. Today, they do not make the pilgrimage to Jerusalem, but they still celebrate the harvest. Schoolchildren make bikurim fruit baskets and wear wreaths of flowers on their heads.

Minor Festivals

Minor festivals make up a third group of Jewish holidays. Since there is no biblical commandment to stop working during these times, stores and businesses may operate as usual. Children, though, have school vacations and special celebrations. *Hanukkah* (Rededication), *Purim* (Lots), *Tu b'Shvat* (the fifteenth day of the month Shvat) and *Lag b'Omer* (the thirty-third day after Passover) are minor festivals.

Hanukkah marks the Jewish victory over the Greek-Syrian ruler Antiochus in the second century B.C.E. Antiochus would not allow the Jews to worship God in their own way. Led by the Maccabees, five brothers from the Israelite town of Modin, the Jews rebelled. They organized an army and won, even though they were greatly outnumbered. The Maccabees reestablished an independent Jewish state and ruled as kings for generations. This holiday has a special meaning for

On each of the eight nights of Hanukkah, a candle is lit in a traditional holder, the menorah.

Israeli Jews today because it stands as a symbol of their own victory of the few over the many.

Today in Israel, Hanukkah is celebrated for eight days. There are games, parties, small presents, special foods, and candle lighting. On each night of Hanukkah, candles are lit in a special holder called a *menorah*, or a *hanukiah*. One candle is lit the first night, two the second, and so on until the eighth night, when eight candles are burning. They are lit in memory of an old legend that tells about the miracle of the oil.

When the Maccabees won the war and drove out the Syrians, they immediately went to Jerusalem. They cleaned up the Temple and relit the lamp that always burned there. Although there was not even enough oil to last for one day, somehow the lamp kept burning. It burned for eight days, just the time needed to bring more oil. Jewish children remember this story when they light the Hanukkah candles.

On Hanukkah, a special relay race begins in the village of Modin, the town from which the Maccabees came. The first runner lights a torch—the torch of freedom and independence—and passes it to the next runner. He passes it on to the next, and they continue passing the torch until it reaches Jerusalem.

Purim celebrates the biblical story of Queen Esther, the Jewish queen who saved the Jews of Persia. This holiday comes one month before Passover, and is a time for costume parties and parades. Many people dress up as one of the characters in the Queen Esther story: the Persian king, Queen Esther, her good cousin Mordecai, or the villain Haman. Children can dress up in any kind of outfit, and it is not unusual to see cowboys, hobos, clowns, and gypsies marching down the streets next to queens and kings.

*For the holiday of Tu b'Shvat, schoolchildren plant trees through-
out the country.*

The last two holidays, Lag b'Omer, and Tu b'Shvat,
are really celebrated only in schools. Lag b'Omer is a
time for picnics and games, and for school trips and
campfires at night for the older children. Tu b'Shvat is a
time to plant trees. This custom took on new meaning
when Israel was being rebuilt by the early pioneers and
later immigrants. Every tree planted meant a victory

over desert and swampland. Today, classes of children go out to the hillsides to plant trees where land has been set aside for new forests.

The Arab Holiday Calendar

Arab children also sometimes plant trees at this time, and this is the one holiday the two groups can celebrate together. But Arabs have their own holidays, too, depending on whether they are Christian or Muslim Arabs.

One of the most interesting things about Muslim holidays is the Muslim calendar itself. It is divided into twelve months, according to the cycles of the moon, though not like the Jewish calendar. The Jews add a month every few years so that the calendar will be correct according to the sun. The Muslim calendar follows only the moon, so that the holidays occur at a different time each year. A holiday might be in the winter one year, and in the fall a few years later. In six or seven years, that same holiday will be celebrated in the summer!

A Time for Fasting—and Feasting!

One of the most popular Muslim holidays takes place at the end of *Ramadan*. This word is actually the name of a month in the Muslim calendar—the month of fasting. Muslims fast during Ramadan in honor of their prophet, Muhammad, who fasted to help people understand the feelings of the poor and hungry. Since it would be harmful to go without food for a full month, Muslims fast only during the daylight. As soon as the sun sets, they are permitted to eat. They may eat until the sun rises in the morning, so the nights of Ramadan are times for feasting and celebration.

When the month of fasting ends, there is a big feast which lasts for three days. It is called *Id-El-Fitr*, the Festival of the Breaking of the Fast, or "the small holiday." *Id-El-Adha*, the Festival of Sacrifice, is referred to as "the big holiday."

Id-El-Fitr is a time for family visits. Parents and children visit friends and relatives and wish them a happy holiday and good luck. The next day the hosts of the day before become the guests. They return the visit and offer holiday greetings.

Sweet pastries and cakes made with honey and nuts are eaten on Id-El-Fitr, and children receive new clothes or other presents. During this holiday, young people and adults often dye their hands reddish-orange with a natural dye called henna. This is a symbol of good luck throughout the Middle East. Women may dye not only their hands, but their hair as well. Henna is part of the holiday celebration, and makes everyone feel festive.

Muslims celebrate the "big holiday," Id-El-Adha, in much the same way, with sweets, new clothes, henna dye, and family get-togethers. However, the meaning of this holiday is different than Id-El-Fitr. It recalls the story of Abraham, the first man to believe in one God, and his son Ishmael.

This story, found in the Koran, the Muslim holy book, describes how Abraham was commanded by God to sacrifice his son Ishmael. Even though he loved his son, Abraham obeyed God. At the last minute God saved Ishmael by substituting a sheep in his place, and Muslims believe that Ishmael became the father of the Arab people. The Hebrew Bible tells the very same story, except that the son of Abraham is not Ishmael, but Isaac.

To remember this story, Israeli Muslims sacrifice a sheep for Id-El-Adha. The animal is prepared by members of the family, roasted over a fire, and then eaten in special holiday meals. Small families may get together with other relatives or friends and share an animal to sacrifice. Whatever is left is given to the poor.

The Druze Holidays

In many ways the Druze people are similar to the Muslims, and they celebrate some of the same holidays. The Druze believe in the Prophet Muhammad, but do

not consider Mecca to be a holy city. Although they do
not fast during Ramadan, they celebrate Id-El-Fitr in the
same way the Muslims do. The Druze also have a
celebration on Id-El-Adha. This holiday marks the
time, in the eleventh century, when the Druze broke
away from the Muslims and formed their own religion.

The Druze also have a holiday of their own to
celebrate the birthday of Shu-eb, an important prophet
in the Druze religion. They believe that Shu-eb, the
father-in-law of Moses, returned to earth many times.
The last time he appeared as the leader of the Druze, the
Caliph al Hakim be-Amri-llah.

Christmastime in Israel

Christian Arabs celebrate holidays in much the same
way as Christians do all over the world. Since most of
them are Greek Orthodox Christians, they follow the
Greek Orthodox calendar and traditions. Israeli Christians worship in their churches on Sundays, Easter,
Christmas, and many special saints' days.

When Christmastime comes in Israel, Arab Christians get ready for a visit from *Baba Noel.* That is their
own name for Father Christmas, or Santa Claus, who
brings presents to good children. Their houses are decorated with Christmas trees, and they have a special
Christmas dinner.

In Jewish cities such as Tel Aviv or Haifa, signs of Christmas celebrations are difficult to find. But in Jerusalem, and in Bethlehem, where Christians believe Jesus was born, there are many churches, convents, and monasteries. Here, different types of Christians celebrate the holiday in many ways.

On December 24, there is a grand procession led by the Latin Patriarch of the Roman Catholic Church. He walks seven miles (eleven kilometers) from Jerusalem to Bethlehem, where he officially begins the celebration. Protestants celebrate with a special service of their own on Christmas Day. Thousands of tourists flock to Bethlehem to attend church masses and services.

Other groups of Christians have their own Christmas celebrations. The Greek Orthodox, and other Eastern churches celebrate with their own procession and mass on January 6 and 7. The Armenian church celebrates its Christmas on January 18 and 19. Each of these holidays honors the birth of Jesus. Because each group follows its own calendar, the celebrations fall on different days. The same is true for the Easter holiday.

Independence Day

Throughout the year, then, the festivals Israelis celebrate are religious rather than national holidays. Israel has only one real national holiday—Israel Inde-

On Yom Hazikaron, *the Day of Remembrance, Israelis honor the soldiers who died defending their country. On* Yom Hashoah, *the Day of the Holocaust, they honor the 6 million Jews who died during World War II. In Jerusalem this memorial, Yad Vashem, was built in memory of the Holocaust victims.*

pendence Day—to celebrate May 14, 1948, the day the modern nation of Israel proclaimed its independence from England.

The day before Independence Day is a day honoring the Jewish soldiers who died defending Israel. It is called *Yom Hazikaron*, the Day of Remembrance. Israelis recite special prayers in synagogues and remember friends and relatives who died.

But when the day of mourning is over, Independence Day begins. It is a time of rejoicing and pride. There are parties, parades, and dancing and singing in the streets all night long. Children carry small plastic hammers in bright colors, which squeak when a child taps them against someone. Throughout the day the noisy squeak-squeak of these toys fills the air as the children walk along and tap each other. The happy sounds are part of the fun of Independence Day.

Even the smallest children have a chance to stay up late at night to watch the celebrations. The streets are decorated with colored lights, balloons, and streamers. Whole families walk together, some with baby carriages and strollers. Young children watch their older brothers and sisters dance the hora and sing: *"Am Yisrael Hai!"*—"The people of Israel live!"

6. Blessed Are They Who Come

For thousands of years, hospitality has been an important part of daily life throughout the Middle East. The Bible tells how Abraham welcomed three strangers into his home. His wife Sarah prepared a meal for them. Only later did he find that they were angels sent from God.

The tradition of hospitality remains in Israeli homes today, and crosses all cultural lines. Bedouins graciously invite visitors into their tents. Although from outside, these tent homes seem plain and bare, they may be beautifully decorated inside with hand-woven carpets and comfortable cushions. Visitors are served small cups of hot, sweet, black coffee from a little coffee pot called a *finjan*, and they are also given treats sweetened with honey.

Bedouin ideas about welcoming visitors into their homes are similar to those of other Israelis. Even unexpected guests are greeted happily, offered coffee or tea, cakes, biscuits, and fruits.

Most Israelis take great pride in their homes, and in their homeland. They enjoy showing visitors what they have built in such a short time in their new country, and how much they have accomplished.

These Bedouin women carry on the tradition of hospitality practiced by their ancestors for thousands of years.

A Shortage of Living Space

Since housing is expensive in Israel, families work hard to buy even a tiny apartment. That small home could represent years of saving, and perhaps a large loan from relatives or from a bank. Because most Israelis own their apartments instead of renting them, they must make a large payment when they buy a place to live.

Despite the fast growth of cities and towns in Israel, living space tends to be limited. A four- or five-room apartment is unusually large, and most children have to share a room with at least one sister or brother.

In the Arab towns and villages, housing often is an even more serious problem. Building new homes is limited by the amount of land available to the town. In some Arab communities, finding a home for a new couple, or even just building a bigger home, has become a severe problem.

Regardless of their size or location, almost all apartments have a balcony. In the spring and summer, the balcony becomes a much-used part of the house or apartment. The family can relax there, entertain guests, and eat meals. Often, balconies are decorated with pots of flowers. Sometimes families use that space to hang their laundry out to dry. Although washing machines are used in many Israeli homes today, dryers are still considered a luxury.

New immigrants, who today are coming mostly from the Soviet Union and Ethiopia, often have no money with which to buy even the smallest apartment. They may have to live first in an Absorption Center maintained by the government. Here they are helped to find jobs and establish themselves in their new country.

Israel has absorbed more immigrants than almost any other country in the world. It costs the government

In this Orthodox Jewish neighborhood in Jerusalem, most of the houses are built with the pinkish stone found in the Jerusalem hills. Each apartment usually has its own balcony.

a great deal to do this, but most of the newcomers adjust well to life in their new land. They learn to speak Hebrew, and become a part of the society.

Family Life in a Kibbutz

In *kibbutzim*, the cooperative settlements of Israel, finding housing is not such a problem. The kibbutz itself provides houses for all new members, or newly married couples. As a settlement becomes more prosperous, each of its members benefits by having more comforts, such as televisions, stereos, or bigger rooms.

If the children live in a children's house, their parents have no need for larger quarters as their family grows. Today, however, most kibbutzim have returned to a more traditional family life-style. Children sleep at home, especially while they are young. During the time that parents are at work, children go to the children's house.

Although kibbutzim still have communal dining rooms where all the members can go in and eat their meals, most families have kitchens of their own. Here, they can cook a light meal in the evening and eat together as a family.

An Israeli Day

Meals in Israel, whether on a kibbutz, in a city apartment, or in a suburban house, are not much different than meals in North America. Israelis have breakfast, lunch, and dinner. The main meal of the day, though, is almost always eaten in the afternoon.

When Israel was under Turkish and then English rule, life was much simpler and slower. People worked near their homes and could easily go home in the middle of the day. Stores were closed from one or two o'clock until four, so everyone could have dinner and a nap.

Today, daily schedules have changed. Most shops are open all day, and workers have only a half-hour or an hour for lunch. Traveling to and from work has become commonplace. Nevertheless, eating dinner in the afternoon remains the custom of Israel.

Some Israelis still nap after lunch, too, especially during the summer. In an apartment house, there may be a rule that between two and four in the afternoon it should be quiet. The residents of the building are not supposed to practice the piano at this time, turn the stereo up too loudly, or play noisy games.

After four, normal activity begins again. Children call to each other on the street. People begin hanging the laundry or beating their carpets. The heat of midday is gone, and everyone comes out to run errands, visit friends, or take a walk.

The Comforts of Home

During the winter, the weather gets colder, especially in the north. Even with temperatures of fifty to sixty degrees Fahrenheit (ten to sixteen degrees Celsius), it feels cold in Israel's stone houses. They are designed to stay cool through the long, hot summer.

Solar heaters are used in Israel for heating water all year round, but they are not widely used for central heating of homes. Instead, gas or electric portable space heaters are turned on for the cold days. At these times, young people may cuddle up near the heater to watch TV.

In summer or winter, televisions all over Israel are likely to be turned on at four in the afternoon. This is the time of day when children's programs begin.

Israel has only one TV station. In the morning it broadcasts special educational programs designed for schoolroom use. At four, many young children watch *Rkhov Sum-sum*, "Sesame Street." It is very much like the American show of that name, with some different characters.

Later, Israeli television broadcasts other kinds of programs. Early in the evening, they are presented in Arabic for Arabic-speaking citizens. Then comes the news and the regular evening programs. Many Israelis watch such popular American shows as "Dallas," "Dynasty," and "Airwolf." Subtitles appear on the television screen in both Hebrew and Arabic.

Youth Groups

For the older children, evening is also a time to go to youth movement meetings. First formed by political parties, youth movements are organizations that now offer young people all kinds of afterschool activities.

Israeli young people go on trips in organized groups to learn to appreciate the beauty of their land.

One of the main purposes of these groups is to teach children to love their country and become good citizens. Members go on trips to learn to appreciate the beauty of the land. Home projects may involve arts and crafts contests, sports events, parties, and dances. Their activities are similar to those of the Scouts or the 4H Club in the United States.

As a matter of fact, one of the popular youth movements in Israel is the scouts—*Tzofim* in Hebrew. The Tzofim are part of the world organization of scouts. Boy and girl scouts belong to a single club and do everything together.

Arab children can also participate in youth groups. There are Arab scout groups, as well as after-school clubs in some communities. Most Arab students, though, return home after school to help their parents in the fields, or to care for younger brothers and sisters.

Israeli Foods

By seven or eight o'clock in the evening, children are in the house. They eat a light supper and do their homework before going to bed. Supper often consists of salad, yogurt or other dairy products, and sometimes eggs, bread, and cheese. This meal is much like breakfast. In Israel, people are more likely to have salad, eggs, and bread for breakfast than cereal and milk.

The main hot meal of the day may include meat and vegetables, soup, salad, and dessert. Among people who come from European backgrounds, the menu and style of cooking may be similar to an American meal. Families who have Middle Eastern origins eat foods that are common throughout the Middle East.

Today, Israelis enjoy a wide range of foods that reflects their country's international heritage. Traditional Arab dishes such as *pita* (flat, round bread), *humus* (a paste made of chick peas), *felafel* (raw chick peas, ground and deep fried in balls), and *tehina* (a creamy paste made from sesame seeds) have become a major part of Israeli cuisine. North African and Yemenite dishes are very popular in Israel, too. Even though it is often hard for Israelis from different backgrounds to learn to live together, it has been easy for them to accept each other's foods.

Middle Eastern dishes have a distinct taste because of the spices and flavorings they contain. Humus is an Arab dish that is easy to make and is a wonderful one-dish snack to serve with pita at a party.

Humus

1 large can of cooked chick peas, drained and
   rinsed
1 clove garlic

1/2 teaspoon salt
1/2 teaspoon cumin spice
3 tablespoons lemon juice
1/2 cup prepared tehina (Tehina can be purchased
   in specialty stores and some supermarkets. It is
   also called sesame paste.)
2 tablespoons olive oil
chopped parsley for garnish

In a blender, chop the garlic. While the machine is running, add the chick peas and blend until they become a smooth paste. Add lemon juice, salt, spices, and tehina paste and continue blending until the mixture is smooth and creamy. If it is too thick, add a bit of olive oil or lemon juice.

Empty humus mixture onto a flat plate and spread it evenly so that it covers the whole dish, but is a bit thicker at the edges than in the middle. Into the middle of the plate, pour a small amount of olive oil and sprinkle with paprika and chopped parsley.

Served together with salad and pita, this dish is a very popular first course in many Israeli restaurants. It can be eaten with a fork, but is best served as a dip.

Pita is a common kind of bread in Israel. It is usually baked in small loaves, which are more like individual slices. Pieces of it are torn off, dipped in the humus or whatever food is being served, and eaten in bite-sized chunks. In the United States, pita (which is sometimes called "pocket bread" or "Aladdin's bread") has become popular. It can be purchased in many supermarkets and grocery stores.

Eggplant is a common dish among both "eastern" and "western" Israelis. It can be prepared in hundreds of different ways. Here is an easy recipe for preparing eggplant. Most Israelis call it eggplant salad, but people from North Africa call it *baba ganoush*, which means "pampered papa."

Eggplant Salad

1 whole eggplant
1/4 cup tehina
1 clove garlic
2 or 3 tablespoons lemon juice
1/2 teaspoon salt
1 small chopped onion (optional)

First pierce an eggplant with a fork in several places. Place it in a greased baking dish in a 350-degree oven, and bake until soft. This should take about one hour. After the eggplant cools, peel, and chop the inside, and mix together with a finely minced garlic clove. Add the onion if you want a sharper flavor. Then add lemon juice, salt, and tehina.

Eggplant salad can be served in a bowl, as a side dish with fresh, raw vegetables, or spread on a flat plate and eaten with pita just like humus.

Perhaps the most well known food associated with Jews who came from Europe is chicken soup. Because this dish is often served on Friday evening in Jewish homes, the delicious aroma of freshly made chicken soup is an important part of the Sabbath for many of Israel's Jews.

Chicken Soup

1 large stewing chicken (at least 3 pounds)
3 carrots, peeled and cut into small chunks
3 stalks of celery, washed, and cut in chunks
2 small onions, peeled
1 tablespoon dried dill *or* 1 sprig of fresh dill
2 teaspoons salt
1 tablespoon dried parsley

Wash chicken and place in a large, deep kettle. Add enough water to cover it. Bring to boil over high heat. With a spoon, skim off as much of the foam as possible, that forms on the surface. Reduce heat and add vegetables, dill, salt, and parsley. Cover kettle and simmer for 2 hours. Remove from heat. With tongs, carefully remove chicken and cool it on a plate. When cool, remove meat from bones and return meat to kettle. Reheat soup if necessary, to serve hot.

The Sabbath

Sabbath (*Shabbat*) officially begins at sundown on Friday. However, its early signs appear in the streets long before that time. Stores begin to close at two in the afternoon, and public transportation stops by the time it gets dark.

People can be seen hurrying home to get ready for Shabbat. Vendors on street corners sell flowers to take home for the Sabbath table. Instead of the usual greeting of Shalom, people say "*Shabbat Shalom*," "Sabbath Peace."

In the more traditional Jewish homes, a special meal is prepared for Shabbat. The Sabbath meal includes holiday dishes that reflect the origin and style of the family. North African Jews might serve a steaming

The Jewish Sabbath, Shabbat, *is a favorite time for a family walk down Ben Yehudah Street, a mall in the newer section of Jerusalem.*

platter of *couscous,* a stew of meat and vegetables over semolina grain. Jews from other Arab countries may offer a lamb dish over rice. Those of European origin often prepare chicken soup and *gefilte* fish, a chopped mixture of carp, whitefish, eggs, and onions, which is shaped into balls and boiled.

The Jews of Israel spend many hours preparing for the Sabbath. Houses are cleaned, and everyone rushes to do the shopping before the stores close. Open markets selling fruits and vegetables are crowded with last-minute shoppers.

Since in most families both the mother and father work, either parent may run errands on the way home. Children also do some shopping, cleaning, or cooking to help prepare for Shabbat.

All of Friday's rush and bustle ends suddenly at nightfall. The streets, which had been packed with cars trying to get home, now become quiet. People begin to relax from a long week of work. A happy holiday feeling fills the air.

In the more religious neighborhoods, synagogues fill up early on Saturday with traditional Jews who spend the morning in prayer. By eleven they are walking home together, dressed in their Sabbath best, to share a lunch of *cholent*. This stew is prepared the night before and kept overnight in a warm oven, because observant Jews do not light a fire on the Sabbath.

Following an afternoon nap, people may go out to visit friends and family. Although they often telephone ahead to say they are coming, Israelis sometimes drop in unexpectedly. Shabbat is a time when "unexpected" guests are expected. They are given a warm welcome and offered the best foods available. The family will greet their guests by saying *"B'rukhim haba-im"*—"Blessed are they who come." It is the Hebrew way of saying "Welcome."

7. *Wake Up!*
It's Time for School

The school day begins early in Israel. By 7:00 A.M. the streets are already crowded with children skipping, running, or walking. Large groups of them wait at the bus stops, with knapsacks on their backs and tickets in hand.

Some are dark-skinned, and others are fair. There are blond, blue-eyed children standing next to friends with black eyes and dark curly hair; still others have freckles and red hair. They fool around, push each other, and shout to their friends, urging them to hurry. All these young people are on their way to school.

Israel has several different kinds of public schools. They are all maintained and supervised by the government's Ministry of Education. Each type of school reflects the needs of one part of the population. The government tries to respond to individual needs and, at the same time, to make education similar for all children.

Schools for Israeli Jews

Secular, or non-religious public schools form the largest school system and are attended by the majority

Sixth graders come outside to play during morning recess at Golda Meir School. Golda Meir was an Israeli leader who became her country's first female prime minister.

of Israel's Jews. In secular schools, the language of instruction is Hebrew. Religious tradition is not taught except where it concerns the history of the country. For example, the Hebrew Bible is studied for its value as history and geography rather than as a religious document. Sometimes it can be a guide to archeology.

Other subjects taught in secular Israeli schools include math, reading and writing, history, nature (which is really a little of every kind of science), geography, languages, art, music, and physical education. By fifth grade, all children begin to study English. In seventh or eighth grade, they can choose another language, usually French or Arabic.

Besides the secular Jewish schools, religious schools are offered as an option to parents who want their children educated in a more traditional way. About one out of seven Israelis is Orthodox, or a traditionally religious Jew. Some parents send their children to the religious government schools because they want their children to know and understand their Jewish heritage.

In the religious schools, children also learn math, English, and reading and writing. In addition, they study Jewish Law and the Orthodox interpretation of it. They learn the exact tradition associated with each holiday, and read the teachings of the great rabbis of the past.

Jewish religious schools teach the Hebrew Bible as the word of God. For them, it is a holy book rather than a history book.

Children who attend religious schools are expected to dress in a certain way. Boys should always have their heads covered with a kippah. They usually wear a small garment under their shirts called a *talit katan*. This small prayer shawl slips over the head and rests on the shoulders. It has fringes on all four corners, reflecting the biblical commandment to wear fringes as a reminder of God.

The girls must wear dresses and skirts, never pants. Their arms and legs are covered according to the code of modesty. This means that they usually wear long stockings, and sleeves that reach at least to the elbow.

The Arab Schools

In schools for Israeli Arabs, the girls may look surprisingly similar to the traditional Jewish girls. Arabs, too, believe that girls should be modest. Although the more modern Arab girls wear slacks and jeans, dresses are preferred in the traditional villages. When they get older, young women may cover their hair. This, too, is a sign of modesty. Most Arab women of Israel, though, do not cover their faces like women in some of the other Arab lands. Although once, young Arab women were kept at home, today more and more of them attend high school and college.

In an Arab school the children study the basic subjects, just as in the schools for Israeli Jews. The main difference is that all classes are taught in Arabic, the first language of all Arabs, whether they are Christian, Muslim, or Druze.

Starting in the third grade, Arab students study Hebrew. All Arab children must learn Hebrew, and most can speak at least some of Israel's official language when they finish junior high school.

As a minority group—about one out of seven Israelis is an Arab—Arab children have special problems.
Although the teachings and writings of Islam, the Muslim religion, or Christianity are included in their schools,
they also must learn about Jewish holidays and read
Hebrew literature. Some Arab parents complain that
their children know more about Jewish traditions than
about their own. They want Israeli schools to provide a
stronger education in Arabic subjects.

Christian Arabs are less concerned about teaching
Islamic culture. They depend on their churches for edu-
cating children according to their own religion.

Education for Druze and Bedouin Children

In Druze schools the children speak and study in
Arabic. They are taught their own religious beliefs at
home, or by example of their elders.

Bedouin children have their own schools, too. They
are run by the Israeli government, and are free to all. The
Ministry of Education tries to keep in mind the special
needs of Bedouins, who do not always have a permanent
home. Field schools, which can move around with the
population, make it easier for Bedouin children to attend
school regularly.

Because of the different groups in Israel, operating
the country's school system can be very complicated. It

A Bedouin boy rests in the desert on his way home from school.

is hard to satisfy everyone when there are so many different needs. Israelis who want a particular kind of educational system may organize their own, private schools for the children of their own group.

Religious Schools and Youth Villages

Certain ultra-Orthodox Jewish groups run their own schools, where boys and girls are strictly separated.

Often the language of instruction is Yiddish, since some of these Jews believe Hebrew is a holy language. They believe Hebrew should not be used except for prayer or other religious topics.

Many churches run convent schools where they teach their individual style of Christianity. The Armenian Christians in Jerusalem have their own schools. They are a small group, and they place great importance on keeping their children together. In this way they can preserve and carry on their Armenian traditions.

Israel has a unique kind of settlement called Youth Villages. In some ways these villages are like boarding schools, and in other ways like kibbutzim. They were originally founded as a rescue effort for Jewish children all over the world who suffered from persecution, hunger, and lack of education. *Youth Aliyah*, or youth immigration, brought hundreds of children into these settlements. They still exist in different forms today, providing a "family" and an education for children who need them.

An Israeli School Day

In spite of the variety among young people, Israeli schools are surprisingly similar in some ways. No matter which school an Israeli child attends, he or she may have some of the same experiences. A Jewish child and

Young people in the first Youth Aliyah group arrived in Palestine from Germany in 1934. With them was Henrietta Szold, an American Jew who helped organize the rescue of Jewish children.

an Arab child living near each other might never meet. Nevertheless, in school they will learn many of the same things, and have a similar daily schedule.

School begins at 8:00 A.M. and continues until noon for the youngest grades. By third grade pupils attend class until 1:00 P.M., and by the time they reach the upper grades they may stay until 1:30 or 2:00.

There is no lunch hour, but there is a morning recess at ten. During this break pupils get a chance to stretch their legs, talk to their friends, or have a snack. Children may bring a small sandwich from home or buy something from the vendors who sell large pretzels, biscuits, and candy near the school yard.

Although they finish school at 1:00 P.M., Israeli children must go to school six days a week instead of five. Each religious group has a different day off each week. It is Saturday for the Jewish children, Friday for the Muslims, and Sunday for the Christians.

Israeli children may start kindergarten by the time they are four years old. The government provides one year of pre-kindergarten and one year of kindergarten for all children, free of charge. These are in separate schools. Four- and five-year-olds do not attend the same school as first graders.

By age six, Israeli children must attend school. In primary school they begin with *kitah alef* (class "A") and go through *kitah vav*. Grades go according to the Hebrew alphabet, and each letter stands for a number. *Vav* is six.

A classroom in Israel is not much different than an American classroom. There are, however, differences between an Israeli school and an American school. An American visiting an Israeli classroom might be surprised to hear the pupils call a teacher by her first name. Students address a teacher as *Morah*, meaning "teacher," along with her first name, such as in Morah Rachel.

Now if our American student raises his or her hand to answer a question, or share in the class discussion, the other students may begin to giggle or look confused. Israeli children do not raise their hands when they want the teacher to call on them. They just lift one finger.

Educational Choices

After sixth grade, most Israeli students attend junior high school for three years, and then high school for another three. High school through twelfth grade has been free for all Israeli children since 1978.

Once in high school, Israeli students may choose one of three basic course groups. *Humani* (literature and social studies) focuses on Hebrew and other kinds of literature, languages, arts, and history. *Re-ali* (practical studies) offers students the opportunity to study chemistry, physics, math, and other technical subjects. A third choice, *Biologia*, provides special courses in biology and in other natural sciences. More specialized high schools offer courses in music and art, photography, agriculture, or trades.

Regardless of the area Israeli high school students choose to specialize in, they continue to take basic courses in all subjects. At the end of the twelfth year, pupils take a series of general subject examinations to test their knowledge. High school students work long

Young soldiers stop for a rest on the Tel Aviv University grounds. After army service, many men and women go to college.

hours studying for the tests, called matriculation exams. In order to graduate, a student must pass them all.

Higher Education

Right after high school, most Jewish Israelis, boys and girls, enter the army. Only after army service will they go on to college. As a result, the average Israeli college student is twenty-one or twenty-two years old when he or she begins university studies.

Many people believe army training is a growing-up experience. In the army young men and women learn to be independent and strong—values that Israelis consider important in their society. The army experience is part of an education that continues in college for those who qualify.

The Hebrew University is the best known of Israel's institutions of higher learning. Others include Tel Aviv University, the University of the Negev located in Beersheba, Haifa University, and Bar Ilan University, which offers religious as well as secular studies.

Students interested in a technical or scientific education may attend the *Technion*, in Haifa, and the Weizmann Institute in Rehobot. In addition, numerous trade schools, art institutes, and teachers' colleges give young Israelis a choice of careers.

Jews have long been known as the people of the book. Throughout their history, they have valued education more than almost anything else. Israel's school system continues a commitment to that value by offering fourteen years of free education to all young people.

College is not free, but it is open to all who are qualified. Arabs, Druze, and Jews study together to help improve themselves and their land.

8. Sports is a Common Language

The big parade that opened the twelfth Maccabiah Games in 1985 was an exciting event. Under the cloudless sky of an Israeli summer night, 55,000 spectators and 4,000 Jewish athletes watched the fireworks. There were thousands of colored balloons, paratroopers gliding down from the sky, and the lighting of the Maccabiah torch. Bands played, and flags and banners flew.

Teams from forty countries marched proudly around the stadium, displaying their colors and symbols. The Maccabiah, the world Jewish Olympics, happens only once in every four years. For Jewish athletes around the world, it is very special.

This major sports event in Israel began even before Israel became a modern nation. The man who first proposed the idea of an all-Jewish sports competition was Yosef Yekutieli, a Russian Jew who had settled in Palestine in 1908. Yekutieli offered his suggestion at a meeting of the Maccabi World Congress in 1929.

The Maccabi Sports Movement

The Maccabi World Congress was established not because there were many Jewish sports heroes, but

The opening ceremonies of the twelfth Maccabiah Games were a special moment for the Jewish athletes who came to Israel from around the world.

because there were not. As a minority in other countries, Jews were cut off from the mainstream of everyday life for many centuries. They tended to concentrate their time and energy on making a living. When they had spare time, they devoted it to the study of their own literature and sacred books. There was no strong tradition of participating in sports or competition.

Late in the nineteenth century, certain Jews took steps to help their people become healthier, stronger, and better able to protect themselves. In 1895 and 1896, the first Jewish sports clubs were organized. Through these clubs, more and more Jews became involved in various sports. Jewish young people began to think about physical as well as intellectual achievements.

By 1912 the Maccabi organization was established, and a few Jewish athletes had competed with their countries' Olympic teams. The Maccabi committee wanted to do more than encourage Jewish young people from all over the world to participate in sports. Its members also wanted to encourage Jewish self-defense and the use of Hebrew as a spoken language.

These goals were shared by the new Jewish pioneers in Palestine. By 1924 the growing Jewish community had developed its own sports clubs and even had a few sports heroes. These men had arrived in Palestine with the new wave of Jewish immigrants. The most famous of them were David Almagor, a gymnast and wrestler from Cairo; Yehoshua Alouf, one of the best gymnasts in Warsaw's Maccabi club; and Emanuel Simon, a track and field star from Berlin.

When Yosef Yekutieli proposed the Maccabiah Games, everyone accepted his idea. The first of these international events was held in March and April of 1932. It was so popular that 25,000 people crowded into a makeshift stadium in Tel Aviv which had been built to seat only 5,000.

From that time on, Jewish sportsmen and sports-women from countries around the world have come to Israel to compete in these games. Many American Jewish athletes earned their first medals at Israel's Maccabiah. They went on to win gold, silver, and bronze medals at the Olympic Games. Some well-known Maccabiah winners are Mark Spitz in swimming, Larry Brown and Frank Spellman in basketball, and Lillian Copeland in track and field.

Israeli Teams and Leagues

Israel has four sports leagues, each supporting teams in several cities and on many different levels. The teams of all the leagues are organized into divisions according to their skills. The top sixteen teams are in the first division, the next sixteen are in the second division, and so on. The best teams play against each other, and the winner represents Israel in international competitions.

International soccer competitions are played through the Asian Games Federation and other Asian associations. Basketball teams participate through the European associations, and are proud of their success. On two occasions, in 1977 and 1981, the Maccabi Tel Aviv basketball team won the European Cup Championship.

Volleyball is also a sport that Israel's teams play on an international level through the Asian Games Federation. But this sport has not captured the imagination of fans the way soccer and basketball have.

Soccer Stars and Sports Clubs

Soccer, known as football in Israel, comes closest to being the national sport of the country. Fans of all ages pack the soccer stadiums to watch their favorite teams. Israelis wait for the results of championship games in much the same way as Americans follow baseball's World Series.

Soccer players on Israel's teams—both Jews and Arabs—have gained international fame. Many sports fans call Uri Malmillian the king of Israeli soccer. Zahi Armeli, Avi Cohen, Eli Ohana, Avi Ran, Moshe Sinai, and Rifat Turk are also considered top players.

Rifat Turk, who plays on the HaPoel Tel Aviv team, is often called the Jackie Robinson of Israeli soccer. Jackie Robinson was the first American black man to play for an American major league baseball team, and Rifat Turk was the first Arab to be a member of a top level Israeli soccer team.

Since then, other Arabs, who first gained attention playing for their own all-Arab town teams, have joined major Israeli teams. Zahi Armeli, an Arab who plays for

Maccabi Haifa, was the soccer superstar of 1984. He led his team to win the national championship. After that, he was named soccer player of the year by two Israeli newspapers.

Armeli went on to join Israel's national team. The members of this team are chosen from among the top players of all the division teams. They play against other national teams in the Olympics and for the World Cup, the world soccer championship.

Israel sent its first team of athletes to the Olympics in 1952 and has been participating ever since. One of the saddest things that ever happened in international Olympic competition involved Israel. In 1972 at the Olympic games in Munich, eleven Israeli athletes were killed by PLO terrorists. The entire world was shocked by such violence, since the Olympic Games have always been a symbol of goodwill and peace among nations.

For Israeli young people, schools and sports clubs are the best place to learn a sport or participate on a team. All public and most private schools offer physical education classes. Soccer is still a boys' sport in Israel, but school teams in basketball, track, volleyball, and gymnastics are available for both boys and girls. Most school teams play in inter-school competitions.

The best young athletes usually join the sports clubs. In most cities these clubs have their own facilities where their members train and compete. They look

These Israeli university students are on their way to play on courts built by the Israel Tennis Centers Association.

for young athletes who have the talent and ability to train for their own upper division teams.

Sports Programs for Young People

Tennis is a fast-growing Israeli sport that has recently become popular. Since 1976, a whole network of tennis courts and training centers has been built throughout Israel by an organization called Israel Tennis Centers Association. The program is funded by Jews from many countries of the world who want to help Israeli children. Designed for youngsters between eight and fifteen years old, it helps keep young people busy and out of trouble after school.

The success of this program has brought Israel to the attention of the tennis world. In the fall of 1985, Israel beat Switzerland in the playoffs for a place in the sixteen-team World Group. This victory qualified the Israelis to enter the Davis Cup World Group competition for the first time. Many of their best players were graduates of the Israel Tennis Centers.

Israeli teachers and community workers have found that sports can help bring Arab and Jewish schoolchildren together. In programs organized by the Israel Tennis Centers and Interns for Peace, young people have a chance to meet on the tennis courts and learn skills together. They play with other children who they might otherwise never have a chance to know.

Tennis is not the only sports program aided by Interns for Peace. This organization, funded mainly by American Jews, has set up a soccer camp for Arab and Jewish boys, and has begun a program for teaching American baseball. Arabs and Jews learn the game together and play on mixed teams.

At a soccer camp organized by Interns for Peace with the aid of American Jews, Jewish and Arab boys learn the game together and play on mixed teams.

"It is a wonderful way to break down stereotypes," explain the volunteer Jewish and Arab coaches who work on this program. They are American and Israeli college graduates who believe that Jews and Arabs must learn to live together and understand each other. "Breaking down stereotypes" means helping people learn what others are really like as individuals. In that way they will not be afraid of others or think that the members of a group are all the same.

A Jerusalem Walk and Water Sports

Many Israelis who do not play in organized sports welcome the chance to participate in outdoor activities. Perhaps that is why so many Israelis of all ages come out for an annual three-day walk around Jerusalem.

This "happening," organized by the Israel Defense Forces, sets up campsites and entertainment centers for the walkers in the hills around Jerusalem. People come from all over the country and from abroad to walk around Jerusalem. Often whole families, or groups of friends, participate together. For some people this event has become something like the pilgrimage to Jerusalem described in the Bible. It ends with a grand march through the city.

Since Israel is bordered by the Mediterranean Sea on the west and the Red Sea on the south, water sports of all kinds have been popular. In addition to swimming and diving, sailing and surfing are becoming more common. Young surfers gather on the beaches of the Mediterranean almost every day after school, even in the winter. On Lake Kinneret, waterskiing is a favorite.

At Eilat, where the water is calmer and the climate is always warm, scuba divers roam the depths of the Red Sea. They explore the beautiful corals and watch the brightly colored tropical fish.

The Massada Challenge

Hiking is one of the most popular activities for young Israelis. Youth groups, schools, and army training units take frequent trips and hikes into the countryside. One of the most popular destinations is Massada.

Massada is a high, barren cliff in the middle of the Judean Desert. Nearly two thousand years ago, it was the site of King Herod's summer palace. During the Jewish war against the Romans, the last group of Jewish warriors hid there. After a long siege, it became clear that the Romans would capture them. The Jews decided to kill themselves and their children rather than live as slaves to the Romans.

This remote, rugged plateau is reached by a steep, winding, pathway known as "the snake path." It is a challenge to every Israeli. Students from all over the world test themselves by climbing up Massada. Soldiers often are initiated into the army among the ruins of Massada.

There are few teenagers in Israel who have not made a pre-dawn hike up Massada at least once. Because of the hot desert sun, the climb must be made very early in the morning. It takes several hours to reach the top. From there the young climbers can see the endless Judean Desert and the hazy blue of the Dead Sea.

Winter sports are not at all common in Israel. Since it never gets cold enough for ice, there is no ice skating or ice hockey. It rarely snows except in Jerusalem, and even there, snow usually melts within a few hours.

Sports in Israel, as in the United States, serve many purposes. Through them, Israelis learn to be part of a group and share in the excitement of competition. The physical activity of sports may also help relieve the worries men and women have about serving in the army. Finally, sports in Israel give some Jewish and Arab young people the chance to meet each other. By playing together they may learn that winning and losing, at least in one area of life, can be just for fun.

9. Those Who Go Down

Because Jerusalem is built high on the hills, the Bible refers to people going *up* to Jerusalem. When Jerusalem was destroyed, and most Jews were forced to leave their country, the city itself became a symbol of the whole land. Jews fortunate enough to visit their ancient homeland were said to be going *up* to Zion. In modern Hebrew "to go up" is the verb that is used when people come to Israel. When they leave, they *go down* from Israel.

The word for an immigrant to the Jewish nation has been adapted from that idea. A person who decides to come and live in Israel is called an *oleh*, or "someone who goes up." A person who decides to leave Israel for another country is a *yo-red*, "someone who goes down."

Leaving Israel

For a long time, a yo-red was thought to be bad. The reasons for this opinion have to do with the early ideals of Zionism. The first Jewish settlers to Israel believed that the only way Jews could avoid being persecuted by other peoples was to have a nation of their own. In order to accomplish this goal, they needed people to come and work on the land. Whether a Jew was a scientist, a teacher, or a laborer, he or she was helping to build the country just by being there.

Being a yo-red suggested failure. Some said it was the failure of individual Jews. They were not ready to sacrifice any material comforts for the good of their people. Others believed it was the failure of the country, which could not attract and keep its own people.

But in spite of the disappointed feelings of some Jews toward those who chose to leave Israel, people did leave. Today, about 480,000 Israelis—more than 10 percent of Israel's total population—live in the United States. Some feel guilty about the choice they have made, or insist that they are just temporary U.S. residents. Each family or individual has a different reason for coming, but almost all of them will remain.

The chance to study in the United States is a major cause for leaving Israel. Although there are excellent Israeli universities, American colleges offer a much greater choice of subjects and more opportunity.

The excitement of travel and adventure also attracts many young Israelis after they have completed their army service. Israel is a small country whose borders with most neighboring Arab lands are closed. For this reason, travel usually means going abroad. European countries are popular destinations for Israelis, along with India and Japan. Still, America offers the greatest attractions—a friendly environment, the chance to work or study, and the opportunity to explore.

The Land of Opportunity

Israel and America have strong ties and many comon bonds. Both countries are democracies in which citizens speak out and even complain loudly about their governments. Their opinions are usually heard and sometimes accepted. In addition, both countries are made up of people from a variety of national and racial groups.

Israelis who come to the United States are likely to find other Israelis to help them adjust to American life. A great number of Israeli Jews come to America at the suggestion or invitation of American relatives. After several years, it is often hard to go back home.

Israel's economic situation is another important cause of immigration to America. Higher taxes and rapidly increasing prices make it very difficult to save money for large purchases. The high cost of such basic things as an apartment, a car, or kitchen appliances adds to the burden of everyday life.

Many Israelis see America as the land of opportunity. They hope to work, save money, and return to

The annual Israel Day Parade in New York City brings together American and Israeli Jews in a show of support for the Jewish nation.

Israel with all the things they need to set up a household. Since most already know at least some English, they do not have to learn a new language.

Once in America they work at many different kinds of jobs, from driving taxis to teaching Hebrew in synagogue schools to coaching soccer. Some find jobs with ex-Israelis who have businesses in the United States.

Often Israeli immigrants are people who came to Israel from other lands and could not adjust well to their new life. They are European Jews who came to Israel as refugees after World War II, Iranian Jews who escaped from Iran during the recent revolution, or Russian Jews who were allowed to leave the Soviet Union.

For many years few native-born Israelis came to America. During the 1980s, however, Israel's economy has weakened, and unemployment has become a serious problem. Perhaps for this reason, more of Israel's upper-class professionals are leaving. Often they come to "seek their fortunes," or to work for an American branch of their Israeli company.

Famous Israelis in America

Two famous musicians, Itzhak Perlman and Pinchas Zukerman, were both born in Tel Aviv. They received their early training as violinists in Israel, but their special talents led them to travel to America.

At age four, Perlman became a polio victim. His legs were paralyzed, and he had to walk on crutches for the rest of his life. When Perlman was thirteen, Ed Sullivan, an American television producer, heard him play the violin in Israel. Sullivan was impressed with the young musician and invited him to appear on his TV show. The American public admired Perlman's courage and enjoyed his sense of humor as well as his skills as a violinist. He was an immediate success.

Itzhak Perlman is known not only as a concert violinist, but also for his charming personality and sense of humor.

Itzhak Perlman remained in New York to attend the Juilliard School of Music. He went on to play as a soloist with many famous orchestras, and is one of the leading violinists in the world today. Although he travels to many countries, his home is now in the United States.

Pinchas Zukerman is not only an outstanding violinist, but also a conductor. Zukerman also came to New York to study at the Juilliard School of Music. He

went on to a brilliant career as a soloist with American and European orchestras, and served as the conductor of the Saint Paul Chamber Orchestra in Minnesota.

Another well-known Israeli who now lives in America is Meshulam Riklis. Riklis was born in Turkey and came to Palestine while he was still young. He lived on a kibbutz until World War II when he left to serve in the British army.

After the war, Riklis came to Minneapolis, Minnesota, and began investing in business ventures. With the support of other investors, he was one of the first to merge several small corporations into one giant one. From his interests in McCrory and Glen Alden corporations, Riklis became a millionaire and contributed to many American and Jewish institutions. He supported civil rights for black citizens in America, gave money to universities, and helped raise millions of dollars for Israel's Emergency Fund during the Yom Kippur War.

Other examples of Israelis who came to America and made their fortune are the Nakash brothers, Joe, Ralph, and Avi. Born in Tel Aviv, they arrived in America in 1962. Ten years later they had combined their names and their talents to form the Jordache Company. Jordache designs and produces fashionable jeans and exports them all over the world.

Ranan Luria's political cartoons appear in many important newspapers. As a boy Luria came to Israel

Pinchas Zukerman, a famous violinist and conductor, was born in Tel Aviv. Today he lives in the United States and performs in concert halls throughout the world.

from Egypt. He went to high school in Tel Aviv and then studied at the Jerusalem Art College. First writing for Israeli newspapers, Luria began to work as a political cartoonist for newspapers in Europe and America. He has published several books and has won many awards. Today he lives in Connecticut.

Menahem Golan, the head of a large movie company in Hollywood, also came to the United States from Israel. He served in Israel's War of Independence as one of the first pilots of the new Israeli Air Force. Golan worked in the theater and went to England to study directing. Back in Israel, he directed several plays and then became interested in films.

Since Israel had no film industry in the 1950s, Golan went to New York University to study and earn a degree in filmmaking. Afterward he returned to Israel and established his own production company. Eventually, he moved to Hollywood, and now heads his own movie company and sometimes directs his own films.

Ruth Westheimer, known to thousands of people as "Dr. Ruth," arrived in Israel as a refugee in 1945 after spending much of her childhood in an orphanage in Switzerland. Her parents had been killed in World War II by the Nazis. She was sent to live on a kibbutz where she remained for several years.

Westheimer came to the United States in 1956. After attending several universities and working in other fields, she eventually became a famous television and radio personality. "Dr. Ruth" is a specialist in sex and family problems.

These are just a few of the many Israeli Jews who have made their home in the United States. Although a few Israeli Arabs have also come to the United States, they tend to become part of the Arab-American community. They do not often present themselves as Israelis. Arabs from Israel do not have to deal with all the conflicts of leaving the homeland that trouble many Jewish Israelis. Both groups, though, often explain their decision by saying that they wanted to live a "normal" life.

A Single Family

Although most Israelis live comfortably in the United States, many miss the feeling of closeness which is part of living in a small country. In America, they are no longer afraid of terrorist bombs and border wars, but they may worry about strangers. The United States seems full of people who don't care about them.

In spite of this strangeness, most Israelis who come to this country settle down and live much like Americans. And yet, many still speak Hebrew at home, follow the news about the Middle East, and try to return to Israel for regular visits.

Today, Israel has begun to accept emigration. Although they continue to encourage *aliyah*, or going up, to Israel, they also understand that some Jews must find their place outside the Jewish nation.

In 1978 Israel built a beautiful museum on the campus of Tel Aviv University—the Museum of the Diaspora. *Diaspora* is a word that means "dispersion" or "scattering." It refers to the fact that throughout history Jews have lived in almost every corner of the world. Exhibits in the museum help Israelis learn about how Jews lived in all these different places. At the museum's entrance visitors read these words: "This is the story of a people which was scattered over the world and yet remained a single family. . ."

The belief that Israeli Jews—and all Jews—remain part of the "family" of Israel is strong. It means that Israel is proud of the achievements of its citizens, even if they no longer live in the land.

The success that many Israelis have achieved in America has reflected well on Israel. Jews who "came down" have helped create a positive impression of Israel throughout the world.

Appendix

Israeli Consulates in the United States and Canada

Israeli consulates in the United States and Canada offer assistance to Americans and Canadians who want to understand Israeli ways. For information and resource materials about Israel, contact the consulate or embassy nearest you.

U.S. Consulates and Embassy

Atlanta, Georgia
Consul General of Israel
805 Peachtree Street N.E.
Suite 656
Atlanta, Georgia 30308

Boston, Massachusetts
Consulate General of Israel
1020 Statler Office Building
Boston, Massachusetts 02116

Chicago, Illinois
Consul General of Israel
111 East Wacker Drive
Suite 1308
Chicago, Illinois 60601

Houston, Texas
Consul General of Israel
1 Greenway Plaza East
Suite 722
Houston, Texas 77046

Los Angeles, California
Consul General of Israel
6380 Wilshire Blvd.
Suite 1700
Los Angeles, California 90048

Miami, Florida
Consul General of Israel
330 Biscayne Blvd.
Suite 510
Miami, Florida 33132

New York, New York
Consul General of Israel
800 Second Avenue
New York, New York 10017

Philadelphia, Pennsylvania
Consul General of Israel
1720 Lewis Tower Building
225 South 15th Street
Philadelphia, Pennsylvania 19102

San Francisco, California
  Consul General of Israel
  220 Bush Street
  Suite 550
  San Francisco, California 94104

Washington, D.C.
  Embassy of Israel
  3514 International Drive, N.W.
  Washington, D.C. 20008

Canadian Consulates and Embassy

Montreal, Quebec
  Consul General of Israel
  2085 Union Street
  Suite 1675
  P.O. Box 184
  Montreal, Quebec 3A2 2C3

Toronto, Ontario
  Consul General of Israel
  180 Bloor Street West
  Suite 700
  Toronto, Ontario M5S 2V6

Ottawa, Ontario
  Embassy of Israel
  410 Laurier Avenue West
  Suite 601
  Ottawa, Ontario K1R 7T3

Glossary

Note: the Hebrew alphabet has many sounds that are not used in the Roman alphabet. These may be hard for English-speaking people to pronounce. The most difficult sounds are the gutteral letters *het* and *khaf*. *Het* is just a little harder than an *h* and is usually written in English as *h*. *Khaf* is a bit softer than *k* and is written as *kh*.

afikomen (ah·fih·KOH·mehn)—a word of Greek origin referring to the small piece of matza which is the last thing eaten at the Passover seder

aliyah (ah·lee·YAH)—going up; the word for immigration to Israel

Allah (AH·lah)—God (Arabic)

al tidag (ahl tee·dahg)—don't worry

baba (BAH·bah)—father (Arabic); *Baba Noel* is "Father Christmas"

balagan (bah·lah·GAHN)—a confusion, mess

B'rukhim haba-im (b'roo·KHEEM hah·bah·EEM)— welcome (for more than one person); literally, "blessed are they who come"

bikurim (bee·koo·REEM)—a harvest festival

Biologia (bee·oh·LOH·gee·ah)—biology; a basic course group in Israeli high schools

b'seder (b'SEH·dehr)—okay; in order

chick-chock (chihk·chahk)—quickly; "hurry up"

couscous (KOOS·koos)—a North African dish made of semolina grain

debka (DEHB·kah)—a line dance for men, popular in countries of the Middle East

etrog (EHT·rohg)—a large citrus fruit, resembling a lemon and used on the holiday of Sukkot

Falashas (fah·LAH·shahs)—the black Jews of Ethiopia

felafel (feh·LAH·fuhl)—a popular food in the Middle East, made with ground raw chick peas and fried in oil

fellah (in) (feh·lah·HEEN)—peasant farmer(s) (Arabic)

finjan (fihn·JAHN)—a small, Arabic style coffee pot

Hanukkah (hah·noo·KAH)—an eight-day festival celebrating the Jewish victory over the Greek-Syrian ruler Antiochus

hasid (im) (hah·SEED·eem)—pious people; refers to a group of observant Jews who follow a particular leader and live as a group

hora (HOH·rah)—a circle dance very popular among Israelis

Humani (hoo·MAH·nee)—humanities; a branch of studies pertaining to literature and art

humus (HOO·moos)—a popular dip in the Middle East, made from cooked, mashed chick peas and spices

ice-café (EYES·kah·fay)—a drink made of cold coffee,

ice cream, and fruit, popular in the summertime

Id-El-Adha (ihd·ehl·AHD·hah)—the Muslim holiday that is known as the Festival of Sacrifice

Id-El-Fitr (ihd·ehl·FIHTR)—the Muslim holiday that ends the fast of Ramadan

kibbutz(im) (kee·BOOTZ/kee·boo·TZEEM)—cooperative settlement(s) where members work together and share the profits equally

kinor (kee·NOHR)—harp

kippah (kee·PAH)—a small, round cap that fits on the top of the head and is worn by observant Jewish men; it is called a *yarmulka* in Yiddish

kitah (kee·TAH)—class; a grade in an Israeli school

Knesset (KNEH·seht)—the Israeli parliament

Koran (koh·RAHN)—the Muslim holy book

Lag b'Omer (lahg b'OH·mehr)—a minor holiday that falls between Passover and Shavuot; literally "the thirty-third day of the Omer"

lulav (LOO·lahv)—a palm branch; refers also to the collection of four kinds of branches used to symbolize the varieties of trees during Sukkot

Maccabiah (mah·kah·bee·AH)—the all-Jewish Olympics held in Israel every four years

matza (mah·TZAH)—unleavened bread eaten especially on Passover

menorah (meh·NOH·rah)—an eight-branched candleholder used to light special candles for Hanukkah

moreh/morah (moh·REH/moh·RAH)—a male teacher/female teacher

moshav(im) (moh·SHAV/moh·shah·VEEM)—farming village(s)

Negev (NEH·gehv)—the rocky desert located in the south of Israel

oleh (oh·LEH)—an immigrant to Israel (someone who goes up)

pita (PEE·tah)—a round, flat bread popular in the Middle East

Purim (poo·REEM)—a carnival holiday one month before Passover; literally "lots"

Ramadan (rah·mah·DAHN)—the month of fasting and celebration in the Muslim calendar (Arabic)

Re-ali (ray·AHL·ee)—realistic; a branch of studies pertaining to science

R'khov Sum-sum (r'KHOHV SOOM·soom)—"Sesame Street"; a children's television program

Rosh Hashanah (rohsh hah·shah·NAH)—The New Year; literally "the head of the year"

sabra (SAHB·rah)—a cactus plant that has sharp spines, but bears flowers and an edible fruit; native-born Israeli Jews

salaam (sah·LAHM)—peace; also goodbye (Arabic)

seder (SEH·dehr)—"order", the name given to the special Passover meal

shalom (shah·LOHM)—peace; also hello or goodbye

Shabbat (shah·BAHT)—the Sabbath; the official day of rest in Israel

Shavuot (shah·voo·OHT)—a holiday that occurs fifty days after Passover; literally it means "weeks"

shekel (SHEH·kehl)—Israeli money

Simhat Torah (sihm·HAHT toh·RAH)—a holiday celebrating Jewish Law; literally "joy of the Law"

Sukkot (soo·KOHT)—a harvest holiday of autumn; literally "booths"

tehina (tuh·HEE·nah)—sesame seed paste

Torah (toh·RAH)—the scroll on which the first five books of the Bible are written; also used to refer to all Jewish Law

Tu b'Shvat (too b'SHVAHT)—the holiday of tree planting; literally, "the fifteenth day of the month of Shvat"

Tzofim (tzoh·FEEM)—Israeli boy and girl scouts

ulpan (ool·PAHN)—a special school in Israel where immigrants can learn Hebrew

yallah (YAH·lah)—a word used to hurry someone up (Arabic)

Yom Kippur (yohm kee·POOR)—the Day of Atonement; a major Jewish holiday

yo-red (yoh·RAYD)—a person who emigrates (goes down) from Israel

Selected Bibliography

Allen, Peter. *The Yom Kippur War.* New York: Charles Scribner's Sons, 1982.

Avinieri, Shlomo. *The Making of Modern Zionism.* New York: Basic Books, 1981.

Ben-Gurion, David. *Israel: A Personal History.* New York: Funk & Wagnall's, 1971.

Chafets, Ze'ev. *Heroes and Hustlers, Hardhats and Holy Men: Inside the New Israel.* New York: William Morrow, 1980.

Facts About Israel. Ministry of Foreign Affairs, Information Division. Jerusalem, 1985,

Eban, Aba. *My People.* New York: Behrman, 1978/79.

Elon, Amos. *The Israelis: Founders and Sons.* New York: Holt, Rinehart and Winston, 1971.

Kluger, Ruth, and Peggy Mann. *The Secret Ship.* New York: Doubleday, 1978.

Levine, Gemma. *We Live in Israel.* New York: The Bookwright Press, 1983.

New York Times. Numerous articles from 1984 to 1987.

Pearlman, Moshe. *Digging Up the Bible.* New York: William Morrow, 1980.

Reich, Walter. *Stranger In My House: Jews and Arabs on the West Bank.* New York: Holt, Rinehart and Winston, 1984.

Shipler, David. *Arab and Jew: Wounded Spirits in a Promised Land.* New York: Times Books, 1986.

Who's Who in World Jewry: A Biographical Dictionary of Outstanding Jews. New York: Who's Who in World Jewry, 1981.

Index

Aegean Sea, 40
Al Aksa, 77
Alexander the Great, 41
Almagor, David, 126
Alouf, Yehoshua, 126
Antiochus IV, 41, 85
anti-Semitism, 46
Arabia, 43
Arabic, language, 76, 115, 116
Arabs: ancestry of, 30, 45; athletics and, 128-129; Bedouin, 17; Bible and, 30; British and, 49; Christian, 15, 18, 63, 89, 92, 116; clothing of, 7, 115; dances of, 32; housing for, 98; invasion of Israel by, 53; Israeli, 35, 66, 145; Israel's independence and, 15, 53, 54; Israel's security and, 27; in Jerusalem, 7-8; Jews and, 37, 46, 123, 131-132; language of, 18, 27, 115; legends of, 77-78; Middle East rule by, 49; Muslim, 15, 18, 30, 89; number of, 116; partition plan and, 56; recognition of Israel by, 59; Sabbath for, 27; Saladin and, 45; villages of, 24; war in Lebanon and, 61-64; in West Bank, 68
Armeli, Zahi, 128-129
Ashkelon, 29
Asian Games Federation, 127-128
Assyria, 40

Babylonia, 40
Balfour Declaration, 47-48, 51
Balfour, Lord Arthur James, 47
Bedouins, 17-18, 24, 96, 116
Beersheba, 17, 20, 34
Begin, Menachem, 59, 64
Beirut, 62
Ben-Gurion, David, 51, 53, 54

Ben-Yehudah, Eliezer, 29
Bethlehem, 93
Bible: dances in, 31-32; Hebrew, 39, 84, 91, 113-114; holidays in, 31; Jerusalem and, 29-30, 136; Jewish heritage and, 29; modern calendar and, 31; music in, 32; names from, 31; promises in, 46; stories of, 13, 29, 69, 71, 81; words of, 20
Brown, Larry, 127

Canaan, 38
Canaanites, 38
Carter, President Jimmy, 59
Chelm, 75
Christians: Arab war and, 45; Armenian, 118; calendar of, 79, 92; celebrations of, 79, 89; in Israel, 15, 92, 115; in Jerusalem, 7; Lebanese, 63; Muslim rule and, 45, 61; Sabbath for, 27, 120
Christianity, 28
Copeland, Lillian, 127

Davis World Cup Group, 131
Dead Sea, 11, 30, 134
Declaration of Independecnnce, 13, 15
Dimona, 20
Druze, 16, 62, 91, 115, 123

Egypt: in Bible, 13; blockade by, 54-55; geography of, 2; invasion of Israel by, 53; Muhammad and, 43; peace efforts by, 57, 59, 64; PLO and, 61; Six-Day War and, 55-56
Eilat, 20, 29, 54, 133
England, 14, 47-49, 51, 54
European Cup Championship, 127
Eurovision Song Contest, 33

foods: on farms, 22; for holidays, 81-82, 84-85, 109-110; of Jews, 12; at market, 7-8, at meals, 100, 104; in Middle East, 105; recipes for, 105-109; at school, 120; summertime, 22

Galilee, 9, 30, 61, 78
Gaza Strip, 56
Golan Heights, 56
Golan, Menachem, 144
Goliath, 71
Greek Orthodox, 7, 92-93
Greeks, 41-42

Haifa, 20, 34, 93, 123
Hebrew language: in America, 145; athletes and, 126; basis of, 70; in Israel, 29, 99; prayers and, 12, 20, 118; in schools, 113, 115, 139; slang in, 76; words of, 42; Yiddish and, 74
Hebrews, 17, 31
Herzl, Theodore, 56-57
holidays: Arab, 89; Christmas, 92-93; dances and, 32; Day of Remembrance, 45; Easter, 93; Hanukkah, 85-87; High, 80, 82; history of, 31; Id-El-Adha, 91, 92; Id-El-Fitr, 90-91, 92; Independence Day, 93, 95; Jewish, 79, 116; Lag b'Omer, 88; Muslim, 89-91; national 93, 95; Pesach (Passover), 81-82; pilgrim festivals, 81; Purim, 87; Ramadan, 90, 92; religious, 79-93; Shabbat, 109, 111; Shavuot, 81, 84-85; Simhat Torah, 84; Sukkot, 81-84; Tu b'Shvat, 88-89; Yom Kippur, 80-81
Holocaust, 50
Holy Land, 45

Inbal Dance Theatre, 32
Interns for Peace, 79, 131
Islam, 28, 43, 77, 116

Israel: Arabs in, 18; archeologists in, 17; border wars of, 35; capital of, 7, 8; cities of, 21; culture of, 32; division of, 40; economy of, 20-21, 64, 140; Egyptian blockade and, 54-55; emigration from, 137, 146; families in, 20, 24, 99-102; farming in, 22-23, 38; geography of, 9, 11-12, 133; government of, 14-15; history of, 16-17, 38, 70; housing in, 97-98; immigration to, 136; Jewish settlers in, 136; languages of, 8, 76, 115; music of, 32-35; naming of, 39, 53; names for, 38, 42; as new country, 12-13, 47; occupation of West Bank by, 56-57, 66, 68; peace treaty and, 59, 69; population of, 12, 137; religions of, 8, 28; sayings in, 69, 72-73; second exile of, 42; size of, 28; stories of, 78; TV in, 102; youth groups in, 104; Zionism and, 46
Israel Defense Force, 57, 63
Israel-Egypt Peace Treaty, 59, 61
Israelites, 31, 38-41, 85
Israel Philharmonic Orchestra, 34
Israel Tennis Centers Association, 131

Jaffa, 29
Jerusalem: ancient history of, 40, 42; Bedouins in, 18; border of, 53; as capital city, 8; Christians' capture of, 45; destruction of, 42-43, 52, 136; holy city of, 42, 93; holy ground of, 45; Jewish rule and, 56; as learning center, 45; Muhammad and, 43; new nation and, 53; old city of, 7; orchestra of, 34; peace accord and, 59, 69; Roman rule of, 42; walking in, 133; weather in, 135
Jerusalem Dance Company, 32
Jewish State, 14
Jews: American, 21, 51, 131; Arabs and, 37, 68; army and, 36, 122; Bedouins and, 18; calendar of, 31, 79; celebrations of, 31; Christians and, 45; clothing of, 7; dances of,

32; education of, 114, 123; emigration of, 146; Ethiopian, 13; European, 140; Hasidic, 7, 32; immigration to Israel of, 12-14, 29; Israeli, 18, 28-29, 35, 66, 79, 115, 145-146; Judah and, 41; languages of, 12; living style of, 22-23; naming of, 40; new nation for, 12-13, 35, 51-53, 66; non-religious, 19, 37, 66, 80; North African, 107, 109; Orthodox, 83-84, 114, 117; persecution of, 28-29, 49-50; prayers of, 33; religious, 18-19, 27, 35, 37, 44, 66, 80, 111; Roman rule and, 41-42; Russian, 47, 124; Sabbath for, 27, 32, 80, 108, 110, 120; sayings of, 69, 72; search for homeland by, 42-43, 46-49, 51-52; Turkish rule and, 46; World War II and, 50-52; Yemenite, 12-13, 32, 105
Jordache Company, 143
Jordan, 9, 53, 55-56, 60-61
Judah, 40-42, 56, 71
Judaism, 28
Juilliard School of Music, 141

kibbutz, 23-24, 78, 99-100, 143
kibbutzim, 99-100, 118
King David, 40, 71
King Herod, 134
King Hussein, 61
King Saul, 40
King Solomon, 40, 42
Knesset, 15, 65
Koran, 77, 91

Labor *(Ma-arakh)*, 64-65
Lake Kinneret, 133. *See also* Sea of Galilee
Lebanon, 9, 53, 61-64
Likud, 64-65

Maccabees, 41-42, 85, 87
Maccabiah, 124, 126-127
Maccabi World Congress, 124, 126

Macedonia, 41
Malmillian, Uri, 128
Massada, 134
Mecca, 43, 92
Mediterranean Sea, 9, 21, 133
Middle East: ancient history of, 41; Arabs in, 49; democracy in, 66; emigration within, 12; fighting in, 35, 68; hospitality in, 96, 105; industry in, 20; Israeli-Americans and, 145; Jewish nation in, 54; Muslims in, 43; World War I and, 48
Mount Moriah, 77
Muhammad, 43, 77, 90, 91
Museum of the Diaspora, 146
Muslims: calendar of, 79, 89-90; celebrations of, 79, 89-92; Christians and, 45, 61; clothing of, 7; Druze break from, 92; holy book of, 77; in Israel, 15, 62, 115; origin of, 43; in Palestine, 45; Sabbath for, 24, 27, 120

Nakash brothers, 143
Natanya, 20, 34
Nazis, 49, 51-52, 144
Negev Desert, 11-12, 17
Nobel Peace Prize, 59

Old-New Land, The, 47
"Operation Magic Carpet," 13
"Operation Moses," 13
"Operation Peace for Galilee," 61

Palestine: Christians and, 45; Hebrew language and, 29; Jewish homeland in, 48-49, 51-52; Muhammad and, 43; Muslims and, 45; naming of, 40, 42; pioneers in, 126; PLO and, 68; Turkish rule and, 46
Palestine Liberation Army, 61
Palestine Liberation Organization (PLO), 57, 60-62, 66, 68, 129
Palestinians, 56-57, 61, 66, 68

Peres, Shimon, 64
Perlman, Itzhak, 140-141
Persia, 40
Philistines, 40, 71
Phoenicians, 40

Red Sea, 20, 54-55, 70, 133
Riklis, Meshulam, 143
Rkhov Sum-sum, 102
Robinson, Jackie, 128
Romans, 41-42, 134
Russia, 32, 51

Sadat, President Anwar, 59, 69
Safed, 45
Saladin, 45-46
Samaria, 56
Samaritans, 16
Saudi Arabia, 53
schools: Arab, 18, 115-116; Bedouin, 116; colleges, 123; daily schedule of, 119-120; Druze, 116; government and, 112; religious, 114-115, 117; Sabbath and, 24, 27; secular, 112-114; types of, 29, 112, 121; uniforms in, 114-115
Sea of Galilee, 9, 38
Shamir, Yitzhak, 64-65
Simon, Emanuel, 126
Sinai Desert, 12, 54, 56, 59
"Six-Day War, The," 55-56
Spellman, Frank, 127
Spitz, Mark, 127
sports: basketball, 127, 129; hiking, 134; Olympics and, 127, 129; purposes of, 135; in schools, 129, 131; soccer, 127-128, 129, 131; sports clubs, 129-130; tennis, 130-131; tradition of, 125; volleyball, 127, 129; winter, 135
Suez Canal, 54-55
Sullivan, Ed, 140

Syria, 9, 41, 43, 53, 55-56, 62

Talmud, 70, 72
Tel Aviv, 18, 20, 34, 52, 126, 140, 144
Tel Aviv Museum, 53
Tel Aviv University, 123, 146
Tiberius, 45
Torah, 84
Turkey, 46, 48, 143
Turkish Ottoman Empire, 46
Turk, Rifat, 128
Tzofim, 104

United Nations, 52, 56
United States: allies of, 66; economic aid of, 28; Israeli immigration to, 137-140, 143-145; Jewish emigration from, 14; recognition of Israel by, 54; sports in, 135; Suez Canal and, 55; Yom Kippur War and, 57

War of Independence, 53-54, 56, 144
Weizmann, Chaim, 47, 54
West Bank, 56-57, 66, 68
Westheimer, Ruth, 144-145
World Cup, 129
World War I, 47-48
World War II, 13, 49-51, 140, 144

Yekutieli, Yosef, 124, 126
Yemen, 12
Yiddish, language, 74-76, 118
Yom Kippur War, 57, 143
Youth Aliyah, 118
Youth Villages, 118

Zion, 42, 46, 136
Zionism, 42-43, 136
Zionists, 46-47
Zukerman, Pinchas, 141

About the Authors

Sondra Henry and Emily Taitz are writers and American Jews who have a long involvement with the state of Israel. Between them, they have traveled to Israel about twenty times since 1955.

Ms. Taitz, who lives in Great Neck, New York, married an Israeli. Her husband, Isaac Taitz, has many relatives in the Tel Aviv area. Recently, they have lived for short periods in Savion and Jerusalem.

Ms. Henry, also a Great Neck resident, and Ms. Taitz have taught many courses about Jewish history. Together, they wrote *Written Out of History: Our Jewish Foremothers* and *One Woman's Power: A Biography of Gloria Steinem*, a Dillon Press People in Focus book.

The two writers would like to share with young Americans the love and admiration they feel for Israel. They hope their book will help American children understand the many problems and challenges faced by this struggling democracy in the Middle East.